THE H FACTOR
of PERSONALITY

THE H FACTOR
of PERSONALITY

WHY SOME PEOPLE ARE
MANIPULATIVE, SELF-ENTITLED,
MATERIALISTIC, AND EXPLOITIVE—AND
WHY IT MATTERS FOR EVERYONE

Kibeom Lee and Michael C. Ashton

WILFRID LAURIER
UNIVERSITY PRESS

Wilfrid Laurier University Press acknowledges the financial support of the Government of Canada through the Canada Book Fund for its publishing activities.

Library and Archives Canada Cataloguing in Publication

Lee, Kibeom, 1966–
The H factor of personality : why some people are manipulative, self-entitled, materialistic, and exploitive—and why it matters for everyone / Kibeom Lee and Michael C. Ashton.

Includes bibliographical references and index.
Also issued in electronic format.
ISBN 978-1-55458-834-3

1. Personality. 2. Honesty—Psychologicial aspects. 3. Humility—Psychological aspects.
I. Ashton, Michael Craig, 1970– II. Title.

BF698.3.L43 2012   155.2'64   C2012-904278-1

Electronic monograph issued in multiple formats.
Also issued in print format.
ISBN 978-1-55458-864-0 (PDF).—ISBN 978-1-55458-865-7 (EPUB)

1. Personality. 2. Honesty—Psychological aspects. 3. Humility—Psychological aspects.
I. Ashton, Michael Craig, 1970- II. Title.

BF698.3.L43 2012   155.2'64   C2012-904279-X

Cover design by Martyn Schmoll. Front-cover portrait by Veer; graph from iStockphoto. Text design by Janette Thompson (Jansom).

© 2012 Wilfrid Laurier University Press
Waterloo, Ontario, Canada
www.wlupress.wlu.ca

This book is printed on FSC recycled paper and is certified Ecologo. It is made from 100% post-consumer fibre, processed chlorine free, and manufactured using biogas energy.

Printed in Canada

RECYCLED
Paper made from recycled material
FSC® C103567

CONTENTS

LIST OF BOXES

ACKNOWLEDGEMENTS

We're grateful to several of our friends and colleagues who encouraged this project and gave extremely helpful comments on an earlier draft of the book: Derek Chapman, Gordon Hodson, Paul Tremblay, Reinout de Vries, and Narnia Worth. We likewise obtained very positive and constructive input on a recent draft of the book from Robert Mackwood, from Taya Cohen, and from two anonymous reviewers. Our book is much improved for these insightful suggestions.

We thank Lew Goldberg and Gerard Saucier for their generosity in sharing the extraordinarily rich datasets from their Oregon community sample and from their English-language lexical research, and also for their insights on personality structure.

We also thank Steve Rubenzer for sharing the facet-level data from his study of the personalities of US presidents.

We'd also like to thank the editorial team at Wilfrid Laurier University Press for all their work on this project: Rob Kohlmeier for his extremely efficient management of the editing process, Leslie Macredie for her great efforts in marketing, and especially Ryan Chynces for his courage in taking on this book and his confidence in working with us. We're also grateful to Matthew Kudelka for his excellent copy editing.

We're grateful to the institutions that have supported our research program. We thank the Social Sciences and Humanities Research Council of Canada for the grants that funded many of our projects. We also thank the University of Calgary and Brock

University for their ongoing support. This book in particular was funded by Brock University's Council for Research in the Social Sciences.

Kibeom thanks his wife and two daughters, who have patiently talked about personality structure over the dinner table many times. He also thanks his mother, his brother, and his brother's family for their ongoing support. Finally, he dedicates this book to his late father, who would have loved reading it.

Mike thanks his whole family—his parents, his sister and her family, and his in-laws—for all their encouragement. He especially thanks his wife for her enthusiastic support, and he dedicates this book to her.

1

MEET THE H FACTOR

Mary and Jane have a lot in common. Both are young women in their last year of study at the same law school. Each grew up in a two-parent family in a middle-class neighbourhood. Yet in some crucial ways they could hardly be more different.

To Mary, the law is like a martial art—a way to defeat opponents by mastering many complex manoeuvres. She chose law as a career because she wanted to make a lot of money, and with that aim in mind she has mainly studied the more lucrative legal specialties, such as corporate law and litigation. To achieve her career goals, Mary has made a point of skilfully ingratiating herself to certain influential professors. By applying just the right amount of flattery, she hopes to make the connections she needs for a good position after completing her degree.

Jane's approach to the law is much more idealistic. She views the law as a means of achieving justice, and her goals in studying law are to help people and to make a difference. She's trying to decide whether to work in the criminal justice system as a prosecutor or public defender, or to work for a not-for-profit organization.

Jane has had some contact with her professors, chiefly when she has asked them to explain some of the finer points of the law. She tries to be pleasant and polite with her professors, but she would be uncomfortable trying to curry favour with them.

Mary and Jane are both single, but both plan to marry someday. For Mary, any prospective husband must hold some prestigious position in society; besides being wealthy, he should carry the trappings and the appearance of a very important man. Anything less just wouldn't be worthy of her. For Jane, these considerations of money and status don't really matter. She's much more concerned with finding a man she can love, and although she might not realize it, this will probably mean a man who shares her values.

As with Mary and Jane, Bill and Dave are similar in some ways. They're both middle-aged men, and both own small automobile repair shops in towns just an hour's drive apart. But again, in some ways they are opposites of each other.

Bill and Dave have entirely different outlooks on how to run a business. Bill's motto could be summed up as "Let the buyer beware": when customers come to his shop, he'll often recommend repairs that aren't really necessary, and he'll often save money by substituting lower-quality parts for those that are intended for a given vehicle. Often, if Bill judges that a customer will take the deal, he offers to do the work for cash, so that no receipts are kept and no taxes are paid.

Dave, by contrast, never deceives his customers or the tax authorities. He recommends only the repairs that are really required, which often means that his customers have less repair work done than they thought they would need. The parts he uses are always as stated on the invoice to the customer. Every transaction is recorded for tax purposes.

Both Bill and Dave are active in their local communities, but here again their styles are a study in contrasts. Bill was recently elected president of his town's minor sports association, and since assuming office he has been quite impressed with his own importance. He's very generous to himself in claiming expenses associated with his duties, and he likes to have his name on many plaques and newspaper articles. Dave, on the other hand, has done a lot of volunteer work for his local sports association, but he often pays out of his own pocket, and he certainly doesn't look for special recognition.

Finally, Bill and Dave differ in their married lives. Over the years, Bill has carried on a series of affairs; from his perspective, a virile and successful man such as himself is entitled to some extramarital excitement. (His wife wouldn't share this point of view, so he must be crafty enough to conceal these adventures from her— and also from any husbands of his mistresses.) Dave, by contrast, has never cheated on his wife. He finds other women attractive, and he could likely find a willing partner rather easily, but he simply couldn't bring himself to betray his wife's trust.

The above vignettes illustrate the opposite extremes of a dimension of personality: Mary and Bill are at one end, Jane and Dave at the other. We call this personality dimension *the H factor*. The "H" stands for Honesty-Humility, and it's one of only six basic dimensions of personality. In this book, we'll tell you about all six of those dimensions—the HEXACO personality factors—but the H factor will be our main focus.

The H factor hadn't been recognized by psychologists until about the year 2000. Back then, most of them believed that people's personalities could best be summarized in terms of exactly five dimensions. Those five personality dimensions, known collectively as the Big Five, don't fully capture the H factor, and therefore they can only partly capture the differences between Mary and Jane and between Bill and Dave.

Research in the past decade has shown how the H factor matters in many aspects of people's lives. It underlies their approaches toward money, power, and sex. It governs their inclination to commit crimes or obey the law. It orients them toward certain attitudes about society, politics, and religion. It influences their choice of friends and spouse. Throughout this book, we'll be explaining the role of the H factor in these various domains of life.

Considering the importance of the H factor, you might wonder why it had gone missing for such a long time—and how psychologists finally did recognize it as one of the basic dimensions of personality. We'll begin with the story of how we happened to find the H factor—largely by accident—back during our days as graduate students.

2

THE MISSING LINK OF
PERSONALITY PSYCHOLOGY

In the summer of 1996, the two of us were graduate students in psychology at the University of Western Ontario. We had known each other for about a year, but now, thanks to the occasional reshuffling of graduate student offices, we were sharing an office on the eighth floor of the university's social science building. Before long, we found that we had a lot to talk about: both of us were fascinated by the study of individual differences—abilities, attitudes, interests, and especially personality traits.

The 1990s were exciting years for personality psychology. The field was recovering from the dark days of the 1970s and 1980s, when many researchers had given up on the idea that personality could be studied scientifically. And UWO was an exciting place to be studying personality: some of our professors, such as Sam Paunonen and the late Doug Jackson, were among the few who had been advancing the field of personality psychology even when it was out of fashion.

The "Big Five" Personality Factors

During those days, one of the most popular ideas in the field of personality psychology was that of the "Big Five" personality factors. According to this idea, the many hundreds of personality characteristics that make one person different from the next—traits from *absent-minded* to *zestful*, and everything in between—could be classified into five large groups, or factors. To summarize the personality of any given person, all you needed to know was that person's levels of these Big Five personality factors.

Personality researchers had good reasons to be excited about the idea of five basic personality factors. From a practical point of view, the Big Five offered researchers an efficient way to summarize people's personalities: measuring a few traits representing these five groups would give most of the information that could be gained—with much greater time and expense—by measuring people on *all* personality traits. And from a theoretical point of view, the Big Five promised to help reveal the meaning of personality: by identifying the common element of the traits in each group, researchers would gather some clues about what causes personality differences—along with some clues about why those differences matter in life.

So, here are the Big Five personality factors as they have been most widely known, with some examples of the traits that belong to those factors:

Extraversion (e.g., outgoing versus shy)
Agreeableness (e.g., gentle versus harsh)
Conscientiousness (e.g., disciplined versus disorganized)

Neuroticism (e.g., anxious versus calm)

Openness to Experience (e.g., creative versus conventional)

Now, keep in mind that these are five *groups of traits*. They're not five types of people. (Really, they're *not* types of people.) In principle, you could measure every person on each of the five personality factors, and each person would have five numbers to summarize his or her personality.

Back in our grad student days in the 1990s, the Big Five personality factors were a hot topic. This five-factor model was making it much easier to do systematic research about personality and its links with other aspects of life. Suddenly it seemed that researchers in every field of psychology wanted to understand how their concepts—from depression to job performance, from conformity to delinquency—were related to the Big Five factors of personality. One of the main reasons for this explosion of research was the development of a personality questionnaire that could measure the Big Five factors very accurately. This personality inventory, developed by Paul Costa and Robert McCrae, was beginning to dominate the field of personality assessment.[1]

Up in our office, we were following these developments with interest. Over lunchtime chats, we often discussed the idea of the Big Five. We wondered about the meaning of the factors. Why should *these* be the basic elements of personality, and why were there exactly five of them? And we talked about the ongoing arguments between supporters and opponents of the five-factor model. To get a grasp of the issues being debated, we did a lot of reading to find out exactly where the Big Five came from in the first place.

One important point, we soon learned, was that no one had *invented* the Big Five factors—no one had simply decided that personality traits should be divided up into these five large groups. Instead, the Big Five had been *discovered* by researchers who systematically studied how the many hundreds of different personality traits were all related to one another.

The first step in discovering the basic factors of personality is to generate a complete list of common personality traits. To do this, researchers search the dictionary and select all of the personality-descriptive adjectives they can find, eliminating only very rare or obscure terms. The next task is to measure many people on these personality traits. This is typically done simply by asking many persons each to rate his or her own level of each trait, on a scale from (say) 1 to 5 or 1 to 9. (Alternatively, the researchers sometimes ask each person to rate the trait level of some closely acquainted person.)

Now, if researchers needed really accurate measurements of any given personality trait, it would be better for them to use a well-constructed personality inventory (see, for example, the HEXACO–PI–R in the Appendix). But the aim here is simply to get some rough measurements of several hundred traits, to find out how much each trait is related to every other trait. And as we'll mention in Chapter 5, people are usually pretty frank in rating their own personalities, at least when responding anonymously as part of a research project. They don't have much incentive to exaggerate good points or minimize bad points.

Once researchers have obtained people's ratings of their personality traits, the next step is to calculate how much each trait goes together—how much it *correlates*—with every other trait.

With these correlations, they can find a few main groups of correlated traits, using a technique called *factor analysis*. (The concepts of correlation and factor analysis are explained in Box 2–1.)

BOX 2–1   Correlations and Factor Analysis

The *correlation* between two traits tells us how much those traits go together in a group of people. Consider these examples.

People with higher-than-average levels of Liveliness usually have much *higher*-than-average levels of Cheerfulness, and usually have somewhat *lower*-than-average levels of Shyness, but they are about equally likely to be above or below average on Organization.

In this case, we say that Liveliness shows a strong positive correlation with Cheerfulness, a weaker negative correlation with Shyness, and roughly a zero correlation with Organization.

Notice that the correlation is based on people's relative levels of each trait, in comparison with everyone else. For most personality traits (and for some other psychological traits, such as abilities), the numbers of people above and below the average are about the same. A few people are far above the average and a few are far below, but most are fairly close to the average.

The correlation between two traits is expressed as a number that can range from –1 to +1. As a general guideline in personality research, correlations (positive or negative) of .10 are considered small, .30 medium, and .50 large. When a correlation is much higher (say, .70 or .90), it usually involves two traits that are very similar, or two measurements of the same trait.

When calculating the correlation between two traits, it's a good idea to measure lots of people—ideally, several hundred or more. In a small group of people, the correlation might be much higher or lower than its real value for the whole population, just by fluke.

Factor analysis is a statistical technique that sorts traits into groups according to the correlations among the traits. Factor analysis identifies traits that correlate with one another and puts them into the same group (or "factor"). Likewise, factor analysis puts traits that are uncorrelated with one another into different factors. The word "factor" originally meant "maker," because the factor represents some influence that makes its traits correlate with each other.

Note that a factor can include some traits that are *negatively* correlated with other traits in that same factor. When this happens (and it usually does happen), we say that the factor has two opposite sides (or poles). The idea is that opposite traits still involve the same underlying dimension. Here's an example: even though "fast" and "slow" are opposite, they both refer to the same dimension—speed—so it makes sense to put them at opposite sides of the same group, and not into two unrelated groups.

The results of factor analysis aren't always perfectly simple. Some traits don't fit neatly within one factor; instead, they might belong partly to one factor and partly to another. And it isn't always obvious exactly how many factors there are: the factor analysis can tell us the best way to classify traits into any given number of groups, but it doesn't always give us a clear answer about what is the true number of groups. These trickier aspects of factor analysis will come into play a bit later in our story.

Researchers started doing these factor analyses of personality traits as early as the 1930s. By about 1960, they were beginning to notice a pattern: when personality traits were measured in any given sample of people—from college sorority students to air force officers—the factor analyses indicated five groups of traits.

During the 1970s and 1980s, Lewis Goldberg undertook some much more systematic studies of personality traits. He studied larger sets of personality traits than previous researchers had done, and he measured these traits in larger samples of people. His results showed five large factors—essentially the same ones as those reported back in the early 1960s—and no others. The Big Five personality factors, as Goldberg called them, were no fluke.[2]

But the Big Five weren't yet the final word on the question of personality structure, for two reasons. First, the Big Five findings that we've described above were based on studies of the English language alone: no one knew whether the same factors would be found if the personality-related words of other languages were examined. And second, the Big Five findings were based on relatively short lists of traits; in the days before high-speed computers, longer lists could not be analyzed. If much larger sets of personality traits could be analyzed, more than five factors might well be found.

Just around the time we moved into our new office, we were reading about the results of new investigations of personality traits—investigations that tested how well the Big Five system worked in other languages and with larger sets of personality trait adjectives. In Europe, various research teams were conducting factor analyses of personality trait adjectives in several languages—Dutch, German, Hungarian, Italian, and Polish. With the recent increases in computing power, those researchers had been able to factor-analyze sets of several hundred adjectives. For the most part, the results of these studies suggested that the Big Five factors really were the basic elements of personality: in each language, the researchers found five factors that matched the familiar English-language Big Five rather closely.

One day when we were discussing these findings, we began to wonder whether the Big Five would be found even in non-Western cultures. So far, all of the factor-analytic studies of personality traits had been conducted in Europe or North America, which left open the possibility that the Big Five might be found only in Western cultures. By conducting a similar study in a non-Western culture, we might find out whether the Big Five really reflected something universal about human personality traits. Fortunately, we were in an excellent position to do this kind of research: one of us was a fluent speaker of Korean, born and raised in Seoul, and had a former professor who might be willing to help us out. We decided to give it a try, and look for the Big Five factors in the personality trait adjectives of the Korean language.

In 1997, we began collecting data from students at Sung Kyun Kwan University in Seoul, South Korea. More than 400 students rated their own personalities on a set of about 400 familiar Korean personality adjectives. On the day we received the data file from our Korean collaborator, we hurried downstairs to the graduate student computer lab and began doing the factor analyses. We waited anxiously as the computer churned through the calculations—in those days, it still took a few minutes to run a factor analysis of so many traits. Would we get results that resembled the Big Five? Would the results make any sense at all? When we made our first quick inspection of the results, we were relieved—and fascinated—to see that the Korean personality adjectives fell into five factors very similar to those found in Western countries. We soon began writing a manuscript about the results, eager to let the personality world know that the Big Five factors weren't just a Western phenomenon.

While we were writing up the results of our Korean personality project, we looked a little more deeply into our data set, by running factor analyses with different numbers of factors. When we had first received the Korean data, we simply wanted to see the results for five factors, so that we could compare the Korean five factors against the usual Big Five. But now we wondered how the Korean adjectives would sort themselves out if we asked the computer to sort them into *more* than five groups. So we checked out the results for six and seven and eight factors. (Remember from Box 2–1 that when you do a factor analysis, the number of factors isn't always obvious; also, you can examine the results for different numbers of factors.) To some extent we were just procrastinating, taking a break from the chore of writing the manuscript. But we were curious to see what would happen.

When we looked at the results for eight factors or seven factors, some of the categories were very small, consisting of only a few adjectives. But the results for six factors were much more interesting. In addition to factors that looked like the Big Five, there was a sixth factor that was fairly large and easy to interpret: on one side, it had adjectives (translated from Korean) such as *truthful, frank, honest, unassuming,* and *sincere*; on the opposite side, it had adjectives such as *sly, calculating, hypocritical, pompous, conceited, flattering*, and *pretentious*.[3]

Six Personality Factors

At first we were surprised to see that there was a large sixth factor. The previous studies of the English personality lexicon had found only five; no sixth factor could be recovered. But we wondered whether this sixth factor might be found in languages other than Korean, so we started checking the results of some recent lexical studies conducted in various European languages. Now, most of these studies had focused on whether or not the Big Five would be recovered. In a few studies, however, the authors did mention briefly the results they found when they examined six factors. In each case, they found a factor that was defined by terms such as *sincere* and *modest* versus *deceitful, greedy*, and *boastful*—much like the factor that we observed in our Korean study. As for the reports that didn't mention anything about a six-factor solution, we contacted the authors directly to find out.

We weren't sure that those researchers would respond to our request for additional analyses, but we were pleasantly surprised. A Polish researcher, Piotr Szarota, replied within hours, and so did an Italian researcher, Marco Perugini. In every study, the six-factor solutions were similar, consisting of five factors roughly similar to the Big Five, plus another factor that suggested "honesty and humility" versus their opposites.

We wrote a manuscript about our Korean findings and published it in the *European Journal of Personality*. Over the next few years, we followed up this research with a lexical study of personality structure in the French language, this one in collaboration with our fellow graduate student, Kathleen Boies. Our French study, conducted in Montreal, revealed essentially the same six factors as those found in Korean and in European languages.[4]

All of these findings made us wonder whether the same set of six factors might be found in the English language too. Remember that in the early English lexical studies, researchers had very limited computing power at their disposal, so they couldn't analyze hundreds of adjectives all at once. We decided to revisit the English language to find out whether all six factors could be found in analyses of larger sets of adjectives. In one study, Lew Goldberg generously suggested that we reanalyze some data that he and his colleague Warren Norman had collected.[5] In another study, we started with our own list of common English personality adjectives.[6] In both cases, we found basically the same six-factor solution as observed everywhere else.[7] By now we no longer had any doubts: there were six major dimensions of personality.

Now, you might be wondering whether there might be some set of seven personality factors (or eight, or nine ...) that are found in similar form across these various languages. We wondered this too, but we found no other personality factors that were consistently recovered. Apparently, there are only six big categories of personality traits.

We now realized that the Big Five system should be revised to accommodate the new results. In some sense, we were too late, because the five-factor model had already become widely accepted by other researchers. Yet these new results indicated that there were six personality factors, not five. So we decided to propose a new model for personality traits, one that would preserve the key features of the Big Five while also incorporating these consistent new findings.

We named this new framework the HEXACO model of personality structure. The acronym "HEXACO" was neatly convenient, because it indicates both the number of the factors (the "hexa" prefix) and the names of those factors: (H)onesty-Humility, (E)motionality, e(X)traversion, (A)greeableness, (C)onscientiousness, and (O)penness to Experience.[8] We've listed in Table 2–1 some personality trait adjectives that typically belong to each of the six factors, both at the high end and at the low end. In the next chapter, we'll describe these six factors in more detail.

TABLE 2-1 Personality-Descriptive Adjectives of Six Factors Observed in Lexical Studies of Personality Structure

H	E	X	A	C	O
Honesty-Humility	Emotionality	eXtraversion	Agreeableness	Conscientiousness	Openness to Experience
sincere	emotional	outgoing	patient	organized	intellectual
honest	oversensitive	lively	tolerant	self-disciplined	creative
faithful	sentimental	extraverted	peaceful	hard-working	unconventional
loyal	fearful	sociable	mild	efficient	imaginative
modest	anxious	talkative	agreeable	careful	innovative
unassuming	nervous	cheerful	lenient	thorough	complex
fair-minded	vulnerable	active	gentle	precise	deep
ethical	clingy	vocal	forgiving	perfectionistic	inquisitive
		confident			philosophical
– versus –	– versus –	– versus –	– versus –	– versus –	– versus –
sly	tough	shy	ill-tempered	sloppy	shallow
deceitful	fearless	passive	quarrelsome	negligent	simple
greedy	unemotional	withdrawn	stubborn	reckless	unimaginative
pretentious	independent	introverted	choleric	lazy	conventional
hypocritical	self-assured	quiet	temperamental	irresponsible	closed-minded
boastful	unfeeling	reserved	headstrong	absent-minded	
pompous	insensitive	inhibited	blunt	messy	
conceited		gloomy			
self-centred					

3

HEXACO: THE SIX DIMENSIONS OF PERSONALITY

As we explained in the previous chapter, there are six broad categories of personality characteristics—the HEXACO personality factors. This means that we could summarize someone's personality rather well by assessing his or her level on each of those six dimensions.

But this leads to the same kinds of questions that we used to ask ourselves about the Big Five. What do these personality factors *mean*? And why should *these* factors be the basic dimensions of personality? In this chapter, we'll try to answer these questions. We'll start by describing in more detail the characteristics of people who have higher or lower levels of each of the six HEXACO personality factors. Then, for each of those six dimensions, we'll discuss the advantages and disadvantages of having a higher or lower level, both in modern life and in the human evolutionary past.

Table 3–1 shows general descriptions of each of the six factors. For each factor, the left and right sides of the page show the characteristics of people who have very high levels and very low

TABLE 3–1 Descriptions of Persons with High and Low Levels of the HEXACO Factors

Honesty-Humility (H)	
High	**Low**
• avoid manipulating others or being false • scrupulously fair, law-abiding • wealth and luxury not so important • don't consider themselves superior	• flatter others, pretend to like them • willing to bend rules for personal gain • want money and expensive possessions • feel entitled to special status and privilege

Emotionality (E)	
High	**Low**
• fearful of physical harm • worry about minor matters • like to share concerns with others • feel empathic concern towards others	• not deterred by physical danger or pain • little anxiety even in stressful situations • don't need emotional support from others • little sentimental attachment to others

eXtraversion (X)	
High	**Low**
• see positive qualities in self • confident leading, speaking in groups • enjoy social interactions • feel enthusiastic and upbeat	• consider self to be unpopular • feel uncomfortable with attention • avoid small talk, prefer to be alone • don't feel lively or dynamic

Agreeableness (A)	
High	**Low**
• do not hold grudges, not resentful • lenient in judging others • flexible in opinions, accommodating • patient and even-tempered	• find it hard to forgive • critical of others' shortcomings • stubborn in defending point of view • feel anger readily when provoked

Conscientiousness (C)	
High	**Low**
• orderly with things and time • work hard to achieve goals • pursue accuracy and perfection • prudent, careful decision making	• disorganized surroundings and schedules • avoid difficult tasks or challenging goals • don't mind incompleteness, inaccuracy • act without thinking of consequences

Openness to Experience (O)	
High	**Low**
• appreciate beauty in art and nature • intellectually curious • use imagination in everyday life • like to hear unusual opinions	• indifferent to artistic and aesthetic pursuits • uninterested in natural or social sciences • avoid creative activities • not receptive to unconventional ideas

levels, respectively, of that factor. Keep in mind that each of these factors is a dimension—a continuum. For the sake of simplicity, we describe people as being "high" or "low" on a given dimension, but don't take this to mean that people come in two distinct groups. Instead, most people are somewhere in between, with relatively few people at very high or very low levels. In fact, the distribution of people's levels on each factor is fairly close to what statisticians call the normal distribution—the familiar bell-shaped curve (see Figure 3-1).

One way to understand the HEXACO dimensions is to consider each as a contrast between two opposite strategies for interacting with one's surroundings. By "strategies" we don't mean conscious or calculated choices. (You could think of tall and short as two contrasting strategies of height, but this wouldn't imply that people choose their own height.) What we mean is that opposite poles of a personality dimension represent opposite ways of dealing with some aspect of life. There are some times and places in which people having the "high" pole of a dimension would be better suited to their environment; in other times and places, the low pole would be better. If instead the high pole of a given dimension was *always* better than the low pole, or vice versa, then pretty much everyone would have about the same level of that dimension—there wouldn't be much variation in that aspect of personality.[1]

Below, we'll be interpreting each of the six HEXACO trait categories as a contrast between two strategies—two opposite ways of dealing with some important feature of life. For each of the six, we'll consider the pros and cons of having high or low levels of the dimension. In describing these trade-offs, we'll consider the consequences of the dimensions in modern life: researchers have

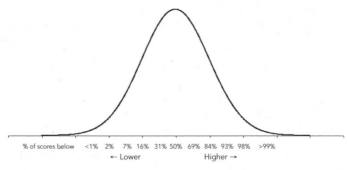

FIGURE 3–1 The Normal Distribution

examined the links between personality and outcomes in various aspects of life, such as career, relationships, and health. But we'll also speculate about how personality dimensions would have mattered before the modern era, both in the recent (historic) and the distant (prehistoric) past.

Engagement and Endeavour: Openness to Experience (O), Conscientiousness (C), and Extraversion (X)

First, consider the O, C, and X factors. Look in Table 3–1 at the descriptions of high and low scorers on each of these three dimensions, and ask yourself this question in each case: Which side of the factor seems "busier"—which one implies *more* activity or engagement of some kind? We think you'll agree that for all three factors, it's the high side. For O, C, and X, persons with a higher level of the dimension tend to be more actively engaged in a certain area of endeavour than are persons with lower levels. What makes the three trait categories different from one another is that each involves a different *kind* of endeavour.

To start, let's consider the Openness to Experience traits. The common element of the high-O traits is the tendency to engage in *idea-related* endeavours: high-O people become deeply absorbed in contemplation of art and nature. They want to understand the human and natural world. They generate new ideas and look for new solutions to old problems. They're receptive to ways and customs that seem unfamiliar and strange.

This engagement with ideas means that high-O people tend to learn, discover, and create a lot more than low-O people do.

In modern society, people who are high in O tend to acquire a wide general knowledge and a large vocabulary. They like to travel widely, exploring new physical and cultural environments. They pursue occupations that demand creativity, whether as an artist or as a researcher.[2]

A high level of O would have provided some advantages in the human evolutionary past. Other things being equal, a person who learned more about other peoples and languages, about different natural environments, and about new tools and skills would have had a better chance of gaining the resources needed to survive and reproduce. But being high in O would also have had some drawbacks. One is risk of physical harm: high-O activities such as exploring new lands, trying new ways of doing things, or expressing unusual opinions all carry some dangers.[3] Another potential drawback is the energetic cost of doing these high-O activities and even of being switched on all the time—of continually thinking and imagining. (The brain accounts for about 2% of an adult human's body weight but about 16% of the body's energy consumption.)[4]

Now let's turn to the Conscientiousness traits. The common element of these characteristics is the tendency to engage in *task-related* endeavours. High-C people organize their time and their physical surroundings. They work hard and long. They pay thorough attention to details. They think through their options systematically and carefully.

High-C persons can gain some important benefits from their task-related engagement. This is evident in several ways in modern life. People high in C tend to perform better in school and on the job than people low in C. Because they are able to inhibit their impulses, high-C people are less likely to smoke, use drugs, or drink excessively. They are also less likely to be involved in serious accidents, and much less likely to lose their money by gambling or spending recklessly. Consequently, high-C people tend to be better off financially and tend to live longer and healthier lives than low-C people do.[5]

In pre-modern times, the work ethic and foresight of high-C persons would have meant a larger and more consistent food supply and better capacity to deal with various disasters. These benefits would have been greatest in environments where working and planning had the *potential* to generate benefits. But if instead there had been little chance to get more food or prevent disasters, then high C would have been less advantageous.

The main disadvantage of high C is probably its energetic cost. People who do more physical work will require more energy to fuel their bodies, and people who make the mental effort of planning and inhibiting impulses will require more energy to fuel their brains. (Interestingly, there is some evidence that acts of self-discipline do deplete the brain's reserves of glucose.)[6] In pre-modern times, when food supplies were less secure than they are today, these energy costs might actually have outweighed the benefits, especially if one lived in an environment where hard work and planning did not always pay off.[7]

Next let's consider the eXtraversion traits. Here the common element is the tendency to engage in *social* endeavours: high-X people assume that other people like them.[8] They're comfortable stating opinions and leading others. They like to make friends and to interact frequently with them. They exude a cheerful enthusiasm.

The social engagement of high-X persons tends to make them desirable partners for all kinds of interactions. In modern settings, high-X people tend to be the most popular members of their peer group, be it a college dormitory, a social club, or a workplace. They're also more likely to become leaders of such groups. And they're generally seen as physically attractive and hence as more sexually desirable.[9]

In the human evolutionary past, people high in X would generally have had more friends, allies, and mates—and a better *choice* of friends, allies, and mates. This network of social resources could have improved a person's odds of surviving and reproducing. But one downside of high X is that it probably carries some important energetic costs, if people who maintain a lively, upbeat state consume more energy than those who are more passive. Another disadvantage is that people who attract positive social attention likely also attract competitive hostility from those who covet that positive attention. This can translate into some risks of physical harm.[10]

According to our interpretations above, you can probably imagine what would be the personality of someone who combines high levels of all three of O, C, and X. Such a person will come across as highly engaged and "switched on"; in contrast, a person low in all three factors will seem rather inert. But because the O, C, and X factors are uncorrelated with one another, few people are very high in all three or very low in all three.

Altruism versus Antagonism: Honesty-Humility (H), Agreeableness (A), and Emotionality (E)

Now let's turn to the H, A, and E factors (see Table 3–1). Unlike the situation for O, C, and X, there's no clear tendency for either pole of H, A, or E to be busier or more engaged than the other. Instead, H, A, and E each involve a contrast between an "altruistic" tendency (at the high pole) and an "antagonistic" tendency (at the low pole). But these three factors relate to altruism and antagonism in different ways.

First, the Honesty-Humility factor: high-H traits share a common element of not exploiting others. People high in H avoid manipulating or deceiving people. They don't cheat others or steal from them. They don't feel entitled to take advantage of people, nor do they particularly want to have more than other people do.[11]

This reluctance to exploit others shows itself in various ways. High-H people are much less likely to commit crimes of various sorts. They generally give others their fair share even when they could get away with not doing so, and even when the others are strangers. They are much more likely to favour ethics over profit and much less likely to be sexually unfaithful or sexually exploitive. (We'll discuss all of the above in more detail in Chapter 9.)

An important benefit of being high in H is that by treating people fairly, one can gain the benefits of future cooperation with others. In other words, when you don't take advantage of others, people generally come to trust and cooperate with you. The cooperation of others can make a more satisfying life in modern society, but in many pre-modern settings this "bank account" of cooperation could be crucial for improving the odds of surviving and reproducing. The low-H person, by contrast, undermines the goodwill of others, thereby losing their cooperation and even provoking their active retaliation.[12]

The cost of being high in H is obvious enough. If your conscience simply won't permit you to exploit others, you miss many opportunities for personal gain—opportunities where there is little chance of suffering negative consequences. The high-H person doesn't exploit others even when there is no chance of being detected and even when the potential victims are powerless to retaliate.

Next, the Agreeableness factor: the common element of high-A traits is a tendency to get along with others even when they may be hard to get along with. High-A people forgive past injustices rather readily. They're lenient in their judgments of others. They're flexible in letting people have things their own way. They're slow to get angry even when provoked.

This tendency to be tolerant and patient has some interesting consequences. High-A people generally report being happier with their marriages—and so do the spouses of high-A people. They also have a lower risk of developing coronary heart disease as well as a better chance of recovery from it.[13]

The main benefit of high A—whether in modern life or throughout the evolutionary past—is that it maintains the benefits of cooperation. In many cases, a person who seems to be treating you badly actually turns out to be a rather nice person. If you have the high-A tendency to continue (or resume) cooperating, you won't miss out on the gains of ongoing future cooperation with that person. But the disadvantage of being high in A is that

BOX 3-1 Herding, Farming, and the Optimal Level of A

Here is a possible example of how the optimal level of A could depend on the relative benefits of cooperation and costs of being exploited. Consider the contrast between a herding society (based on livestock) and a farming society (based on crops). Livestock such as sheep and cattle are very mobile, so it's easy for rustlers to round them up and drive them away; to deter this potentially disastrous kind of exploitation, herding societies favour lower levels of A. In contrast, low A is less advantageous in a farming society: it's much harder for a would-be thief to harvest a field of crops and carry them away, and there may also be more opportunities for cooperation (think of the old-fashioned barn-raising bees). Some researchers have used the contrast between herding and farming societies to explain the differences between the cultures of White settlers in the southern and northern United States: the South, whose upland areas were settled mainly by herders, has been known for its "culture of honour," in which minor insults can spark feuds.[14]

it also allows you to continue cooperating with people who truly are trying to exploit you.[15]

The H and A factors thus represent two distinct aspects of the tendency to be cooperative: high-H people cooperate with you even when they could get away with exploiting you; high-A people cooperate with you even when you are not really cooperating fully with them. Low-H people undermine cooperation by taking unfair advantage of you, and low-A people undermine cooperation by being too quick to decide that you're taking advantage of them.

Finally, the Emotionality factor: the common element of the E traits is that they promote the survival of oneself and one's kin. People high in E avoid physical dangers. They worry about potential harms both to themselves and to their families. They seek help and support in times of need. They feel strong empathy and attachment toward their family and close friends.

The self- and kin-preservation associated with the E factor shows up in several ways. For example, very high-E people are at risk for what psychologists call "separation anxiety disorder."[16] Although this disorder is usually diagnosed in children, it occurs in adults too: some adults dread being apart for even one night from their spouse or child and worry obsessively about unlikely harms that might befall those persons, such as a freak accident or a kidnapping. High-E persons are also more likely to develop phobias—that is, excessively strong fears of physical dangers, such as animals, blood and injections, collisions and falls, and closed spaces.[17] Conversely, very low-E people can have the opposite problems: some of them are indifferent to family ties and incapable of romantic love. Some of them suffer injury or even death because—being undeterred by the prospect of physical harm and pain—they expose themselves to great dangers both at work and at play.

The benefit of high E is therefore the reduced likelihood that serious harm will befall oneself and one's kin. The cost, however, is that high-E persons (and their kin) forgo the potential gains from activities that carry risks to the well-being of oneself or one's kin. In the human evolutionary past, the ideal level of E would have depended on the local environment. For example, if the only way to make a living was to carry out some dangerous task, lower E would have been better. Or, if there were many avoidable dangers to oneself and one's offspring, higher E would have been better.

The relative value of higher versus lower E also depends on one's sex. Throughout the human past, the survival of a child depended more on its mother's survival than on its father's.[18] And for a woman, the heavy biological cost of pregnancy and lactation means that having another child is a much more difficult proposition than it is for a man. (Moreover, a woman rarely has any doubts about which children are her own and which children aren't, whereas a man has less certainty on both counts.) Consistent with these facts, the average level of E is consistently higher for women than for men. This difference is not huge— there's a lot of overlap between the sexes in their levels of E, about as much as there is for height—but it's found reliably across cultures as different as the United States and Turkey, or Korea and the Netherlands.

As we mentioned earlier, the E factor promotes strong feelings of empathic concern and emotional attachment, which in turn promote altruism (and inhibit aggression) toward one's kin. In short, high-E people have a strong inclination toward *kin altruism*. Now, suppose that an individual has not only a high level of E but also high levels of both H and A—the ingredients of cooperation, or *reciprocal altruism*. Such a person will be highly altruistic all-around—basically, a very nice person. Conversely, a person low in E, H, and A will be highly antagonistic—a very nasty person.

BOX 3-2 Personality and Altruism: H as the Missing Link

When we noticed the H factor in studies of personality trait words, we finally understood the answer to a problem that had nagged at us for several years. Back in 1996, when we started working together, we were trying to understand the Big Five Agreeableness and Emotional Stability factors in terms of what biologists call "kin altruism" (i.e., a tendency to be protective and solicitous of your family members and other people who are like family) and "reciprocal altruism" (i.e., a tendency to cooperate with others in general). Basically, we believed that "sentimental" traits (such as empathy and emotional attachment) should promote kin altruistic behaviour, whereas "patient" traits (such as tolerance and even temper) should promote reciprocally altruistic behaviour.

When the studies of various languages showed that sentimental traits and patient traits formed neat factors of their own—the E and A factors, respectively—this made perfect sense to us. But the finding of an H factor solved an even bigger problem. Back when we were developing our ideas about personality traits in relation to kin altruism and reciprocal altruism, we realized that something was missing. According to theoretical biology, "reciprocal altruism" should involve two quite distinct kinds of traits. Being a tolerant, patient person makes you a good partner for cooperation, because you aren't always getting unduly angry at other people. At the same time, being an honest, fair-minded person also makes you a good partner for cooperation, because you aren't always trying to cheat other people.

These latter tendencies didn't have a place of their own in the Big Five model. But when the sixth factor was found, everything fell neatly into line: there was one factor for traits that promote kin altruism (E), one factor for the "patient" kind of reciprocal altruism (A), and one factor for the "fair" kind of reciprocal altruism (H).

As we mentioned above, people who are high in all three of these factors are very nice people. This can also be seen in the results of lexical studies of personality structure, for traits that describe an overall "nice" tendency—for example, *sympathetic* or *soft-hearted*—tend to fall partly in the E trait category, partly in the H trait category, and partly in the A trait category.

In this chapter, we've tried to explain the meaning of the HEXACO personality factors—why these six dimensions are important, and why people differ so widely in these aspects of personality. We've argued that each dimension can be seen in terms of two opposing strategies for dealing with one's surroundings: depending on where and when a person is living, a higher level of a given dimension may work better than a lower level, or vice versa.

So far, however, we've considered each personality factor in isolation from the others. In the next chapter, we'll explore the personalities of people who exhibit various *combinations* of the personality dimensions. We'll be focusing on people who have low levels of the H factor in combination with high or low levels of the other five dimensions.

But before you read about these varieties of low-H people, you might be interested in a couple of fundamental questions about personality: Do people have different personalities because of the genes they inherit or because of environments they experience? And how much do people's personalities change throughout their lives? We examine these questions in Box 3–3 and Box 3–4.

BOX 3-3   Nature and Nurture

Suppose that we take a large group of adults from any modern, developed country. These adults grew up in families that differed widely in their levels of income, education, and religiosity, and in their styles of raising children. But these adults still have much in common: they're all from the same ethnic group and the same generation, and they all went to similar schools and grew up in broadly similar communities. None of them experienced any really severe abuse or neglect when growing up, and none of them were desperately poor.

The adults of this group will show the full variety of personalities. For any of the six personality dimensions, some will be very high, others very low, and most somewhere in between.

But *why* are they so different in personality? Is it mainly because of nature—differences in the genes they inherited? Or is it mainly because of nurture—differences in the families and households they grew up in? The answer is one of the most striking discoveries of personality psychology: genes are heavily involved in personality differences, rearing environments hardly at all.

How do we know? Researchers have figured this out by measuring the personalities of various kinds of relatives, to find out how similar those different kinds of relatives typically are. For example, suppose we measure many pairs of *identical* twins (who share 100% of their genes—they're genetically identical). And suppose we do the same with many pairs of *fraternal* twins (who share 50% of their genes—the same as for regular, non-twin siblings). If identical twins tend to be more similar to each other in personality than are fraternal twins, this suggests that heredity (nature) has an influence on personality. (Here we're talking about the genes that actually differ from one person to the next. We're ignoring all of the genes—the vast majority—that are identical for all human beings.)

As another example, suppose that we measure many pairs of biological siblings who were raised *together* (the usual situation). And suppose we do the same with many pairs of biological siblings who were raised *apart* (perhaps due to adoption or divorce). If the siblings raised together tend to be more similar to each other in personality, this suggests that the rearing environment (nurture) has an influence on personality.

For one last example, suppose that we measure many pairs of siblings who are biologically unrelated (as happens when a family adopts one or more children). If these siblings tend to be at all similar in personality, this suggests that the rearing environment is also involved.

When researchers do these kinds of studies, here's what they find:[19]

- On average, identical twins are very similar in personality, and about twice as similar as fraternal twins.
- On average, biological siblings are only modestly similar in personality, but it doesn't matter if they were raised together or apart.
- On average, adoptive relatives aren't similar at all in personality—no more than any other biologically unrelated people.

All of this tells us that differences in people's genes do contribute to differences in their personalities and that differences in their rearing environments do not. The best recent estimates are that personality differences are about two-thirds due to genetic differences and almost not at all due to differences in early household environment. This means that if two people have identical genes, they'll likely have rather similar personalities even if they're raised in different households. Also, if two people have entirely different genes, they'll have quite different personalities even if they're raised in the same household. Keep in mind, though, that these studies probably include very few people who had been severely abused or neglected as children. If there were many such people in the research samples, the results might well show some effects of the rearing environment.[20]

By the way, these findings don't mean that there must be one specific gene, or even a few specific genes, that cause people to have higher or lower levels of any given personality factor. Research thus far suggests that personality differences are caused by the combined effects of very many genes, each of which has only a small effect on its own. As for exactly how those genes influence personality—how they act through the workings of our brains—it will likely be a long time before researchers have much more than a superficial understanding.

But if personality differences between people are two-thirds due to genetic differences and not at all due to household environment differences, what about the other one-third of personality differences? Well, even though your personality as an adult probably doesn't depend much on the household or family in which you were raised, it is possible that your experiences while growing up still had some effect. Researchers have suggested some early experiences that might influence adult personality:

• Peer, or friendship, groups during adolescence: people might become more similar to their friends in some aspects of personality (thereby fitting in with their peers), or they might become more distinct from their friends in other aspects (thereby being unique among their peers).[21]

- Birth order—more specifically, a person's age rank among the siblings raised in his or her family: for example, it has been suggested that later-born children may be more rebellious than earlier-born children.[22]

Research studies conducted so far suggest that these effects are likely to be small,[23] but taken together and in combination with various other influences, they should account for the one-third of personality variation that isn't accounted for by genetic differences.

BOX 3–4 Does Personality Change?

The question of whether personality changes is actually two different questions. First, does the average person change in some predictable ways throughout his or her lifespan? And second, do people change in comparison with the average person of their own age group? To see the difference between these questions, consider athletic ability: obviously, the average adult becomes less athletic between age 20 and age 60, but this doesn't mean that the *most* athletic 20-year-olds end up as the *least* athletic 60-year-olds.

To get a picture of how the typical person develops, researchers have measured people's personalities at intervals of several years. Their findings show that most people become somewhat higher in the A, C, and H factors of personality between their teens and their forties. The difference isn't large—in fact, there are many teenagers who have high levels of these factors, and many middle-agers who have low levels. But the trend is for people to be more responsible, better socialized citizens after young adulthood than they were before it.[24]

It isn't yet clear why these changes happen. Perhaps as people progress through young adulthood, changes occur in their biological predisposition for these personality characteristics. Or perhaps the typical changes in life's circumstances during young adulthood—career, marriage, children, homeownership—simply bring out more of the behaviours associated with these aspects of personality.

Researchers have used the same data to get a picture of how people change in comparison with other people of their own age cohort. These data generally show that people's personality trait levels—compared with the levels of other people from their own age cohort—are highly consistent even over many years. For any given personality trait, a person's level at (say) 30 years old will very likely be similar to his or her level five decades later, when he or she is 80 years old. (This degree of consistency is somewhat lower during adolescence and young adulthood, when there is a bit more shifting in people's levels of the major personality traits.)[25] Although some people do show important changes in their personality trait levels, most people don't.

4

A FIELD GUIDE TO LOW-H PEOPLE

So far in this book, we've been describing all six of the major dimensions of personality. In the remaining chapters, we'll focus mostly on the H factor. The main reason for this special attention is that the H factor has such a powerful influence on so many aspects of people's lives—on their choice of friends and romantic partners, on their sexual behaviour, on their approach toward money and power, on their political and religious views, and so on. But before we discuss these expressions of the H factor, we'll describe the personalities of low-H people in more detail. We could just as well focus on high-H people, but in many ways it's more interesting to consider people at the low pole of this dimension, given that it's low-H people whose behaviour often has such dramatic—and harmful—consequences.

We described the core characteristics of low-H persons in the previous chapter. But low-H people can differ greatly from one another, depending on their levels of the five other personality factors. Here we'll explore some of the main variations on the low-H personality by exploring the key characteristics of people who combine low H with high or low levels of each of the other personality factors. By taking low H in combination with each of the other factors in turn, we hope to show the main ways in which low-H people express their personalities.

When reading the profiles below, you should keep some important points in mind. First of all, a person who is very low in H could match several of these descriptions rather well. Also, the accuracy of any given description for any given person is not all-or-nothing—it's a matter of degree, depending on just how high or how low the person's levels of the factors happen to be. And finally, you should be prepared to find that some of these profiles will be at least slightly reminiscent of your own personality: you'll probably see some hints of your own tendencies in at least one or two of these descriptions. But this will be true for nearly every-one—and that includes your authors.

Low H, Low E: Greed without Fear—or Pity

It's often said that risk taking is governed by greed and fear. Well, people who combine low Honesty-Humility with low Emotionality have a whole lot of greed and not much fear: they're hungry for money and power, and their appetite isn't spoiled by the risk of physical harm. Accordingly, it's low-H, low-E people who take the biggest chances in pursuit of fame and fortune. They want to win it all or die trying.

We call this tendency "status-driven risk taking," and it gets expressed in several ways.[1] For example, people who are low in both H and E will be the ones most tempted by very high-paying but dangerous jobs. If you were to advertise for mercenary soldiers, offering huge rewards for fighting in some deadly conflict, you would probably get a lot of low-H, low-E applicants. If there were a modern-day gold rush in some remote and very hazardous corner of the world, the same kind of crowd would show up.

The combination of low H and low E is also relevant to status-driven risk taking in more common situations. People who like to compete in showing off their bravery tend to be low-H, low-E people. Think of the game of "chicken." Think of barroom brawls. The competitors in these contests are almost always men—usually *young* men. This fact is probably due in large part to the differences between men and women in their levels of E and H. Compared with women, men tend to be considerably lower in E and somewhat lower in H, so the large majority of very low-H, very low-E people are men. And given that competition tends to be strongest between members of the same sex, it isn't hard to see why almost all the people killed while competing for status have been men: rates of homicide and accidental deaths are consistently much higher for men than for women, especially during young adulthood, a stage of life when competition is particularly intense.[2]

This isn't to say that personality—in particular the H and E factors—explains everything about status-driven risk taking, let alone homicides and fatal accidents. The cultural context also matters: when people live in a "winner-take-all" society marked by strong inequalities of income, the level of status-driven risk taking will be high. This is even more likely when a society is polygynous—that is, when some men have several wives and other men have no wives at all. Extreme inequalities encourage men to exhibit more low-H, low-E behaviours, which in turn elicits status-driven risk taking even from men who aren't by nature especially low in H or low in E.

In pursuing wealth and status, people with low levels of H and E are willing to put themselves at risk; they also don't care if they put other people at risk too. To put it bluntly, low-H, low-E people are cold and callous. They don't feel much empathy or pity; they're simply unmoved by the suffering of other people and aren't interested in helping people who are in really desperate straits. Likewise, low-H, low-E people don't see any reason to avoid harming others in pursuing their own ends. If they have to step on you to achieve their goals, that's tough—you should just suck it up. As you can see, people low in H and E are not very nice. Those who are also low in A have pretty much the complete package for being an all-around nasty person.

Low H, High E: Weaseling and Whining

Compared with people who are low in both Honesty-Humility and Emotionality, people who combine low H with high E are not nearly so dangerous. They are much more fearful, so they don't do so much status-driven risk taking. They are also much less insensitive, so they usually don't treat people in quite such a hard-hearted way.

But the combination of low H and high E can still cause problems. Low-H, high-E people will try to exploit others, but they will do so in subtle, sneaky ways in order to avoid any confrontation or other risk of harm. A low-H, low-E person would risk a real fight; a low-H, high-E person would prefer to sneak away. When watching a low-H, high-E person in action, the words "weasel" and "coward" come to mind. In some ways, the combination of low H and high E is exactly opposite to the popular image of a hero. In the typical action movie, the good guy—usually a police officer or a secret agent—is always tough and brave. This high-H, low-E character is not a particularly sensitive soul, but he—virtually always a "he"—is incorruptible, with a strong sense of justice.

People who combine low H with high E may use their own weakness—or at least the exaggeration of their weakness—as a means of getting more than their share of various benefits. Think of the university student who exaggerates illnesses or other problems to request extra exam time and extended essay deadlines. Think of the spouse who expects to be waited on or to be showered with gifts. The blend of low H and high E is not very scary, but with its weaseling and whining, it can certainly be annoying.

BOX 4–1   Of Conquistadors and Sweetheart Swindlers

Many of the most famous—or most infamous—figures of history showed the combination of low H and low E. Some of the best examples are the Spanish conquistadors of the 16th century. Among these tough, greedy men were the Pizarro brothers—Francisco, Gonzalo, Juan, and Hernando. Under Francisco's leadership, all four brothers took part in the conquest of the Inca Empire in 1532. The enterprise was motivated purely by greed: the brothers hoped to replicate the exploits of Hernán Cortés (a second cousin), who conquered the Aztec Empire and looted its wealth. The Pizarros' operation was extremely risky, as their force of fewer than 200 men was invading an empire that could field tens of thousands of warriors. But as a result of several advantages—including horses, steel weapons, and a concurrent smallpox outbreak among the native population—the Spanish defeated the Incas, often by resorting to trickery and surprise. The Pizarro brothers and their comrades then set about plundering the Inca Empire, seizing vast stores of gold and silver. They ruled the conquered territories as brutal tyrants, raping and pillaging; their cruelty provoked a rebellion in which Juan was killed. Francisco betrayed his erstwhile partner, Diego de Almagro, and was later killed by Almagro's son. Greedy for still more riches, Gonzalo undertook an extremely dangerous expedition into the Amazon in search of the legendary (and non-existent) city of gold, El Dorado; most of his men died or deserted, but Gonzalo survived. Later, when the Spanish king's viceroy in Peru enforced some new laws aimed at preventing exploitation of the native inhabitants, Gonzalo rebelled and was subsequently executed. Only Hernando survived to old age, but even he was imprisoned in Spain for twenty years.

The conquistadors in general, and the Pizarros in particular, showed extremely low levels both of H (in their greed and deceit) and of E (in their fearlessness and toughness). The Pizarros and other conquistadors were excellent (albeit rather extreme) examples of the low-H, low-E combination; many other historical figures showed this same blend of traits. People who combine the exploitiveness of low H with the toughness of low E have the potential to create a great deal of mayhem if they survive long enough. In contrast, people who combine low H with *high* E are much more risk-averse and not nearly so callous; thus, in spite of their selfish motivations, they are much less likely to make themselves famous.

Still, one might wonder whether there are any spectacular exploits that would be especially well suited to low-H, high-E persons. One superficially plausible candidate is the so-called sweetheart swindler scam. The swindler, a woman, approaches an elderly man, befriends him, and eventually pretends to fall in love with him. The typical story she tells the victim is cliché:

she is a single mother with a miserable life story and lots of debt, and therefore she needs financial help to support her children (who, for good measure, may be seriously ill). If everything goes right, she takes the victim's money until there is nothing left. The pattern seems to suggest that this is a crime suited to a low-H woman who also has high-E traits of dependence and vulnerability.

We doubt, however, that sweetheart swindlers of this kind are high in the E factor. These con artists pretend to be weak and dependent to get what they want, but in reality they are very tough customers. Not only are they extremely callous, turning very cold toward their victims once the money is gone, but they are also rather fearless, willingly taking on the risk of going to prison for fraud. A person who combines low H with high E would likely be deterred by the fear of being caught and might even find it hard to remain emotionally detached from the victim. Such a person would be inclined to commit only lower-level, less risky antisocial acts—such as keeping the cash in a lost wallet, exaggerating medical symptoms for time off work, or secretly spreading rumours about persons they don't like. It's much less likely that the low-H, high-E person would carry out anything as bold and as cold as the sweetheart swindler scam.

Low H, High X: Narcissism Run Wild

People who combine low Honesty-Humility with high eXtraversion are the kind of people who get your attention. And as far as they're concerned, this is exactly how it should be: low-H, high-X people are narcissists. They stand in awe of their own greatness, and they think you should too.

Low-H, high-X persons see themselves as born leaders, and in some sense they are quite right. Their high X means they're comfortable when meeting new people and confident when speaking out in large-group settings. For these people, being the focus of attention is exhilarating, not exhausting. But their low H means that they passionately want to rule over others: they crave power, and they feel entitled to it as if by divine right. They manipulate others to achieve high status, and once they get it they use it for personal advantage—financial, sexual, or otherwise. The low-H, high-X person loves to dominate others: for them, being the alpha male or the alpha female is what it's all about.

It's easy to poke fun at these people, and in fact we recommend it highly. But you still have to take them seriously, because the low-H, high-X combination can be formidable. Low-H, high-X persons have a charm and charisma that attract a crowd of admiring followers. (And this magnetism can only be amplified by any other asset they might happen to have—good looks or athleticism or intelligence, or personality traits such as high O or high C.) Their boldness and energy in social interactions are blended with cunning and guile, making them skilled political operators who often succeed in navigating their way into positions of power.

But as you might guess, not everyone becomes (or stays) enthralled with the leadership of low-H, high-X persons. Leaders who are low in H and high in X are tirelessly self-aggrandizing and self-promoting, without intrinsic concern for the well-being of the people or the organization that is under their leadership. Some people see this, and resent it. When low-H, high-X leaders break too many rules and alienate too many people, all of their ruthless charm won't be enough to prevent a hard fall.

The narcissism of the low-H, high-X person isn't restricted to the realm of leadership. The combination of high X and low H is a perfect recipe for showing off: if they've got it, you can bet they'll flaunt it. They like to regale you with stories that reveal their superior status and the remarkable talents and achievements that go with it. (If they're good at this, it might not even be particularly obnoxious, and you might even be entertained by it.) They display the material evidence of their greatness, drawing attention with the trappings of whatever status and achievement they possess.

Low-H, high-X people are immodest, and not only in the general sense of boastfulness and ostentation. They're equally immodest in the more specific sense of being sexually provocative and seductive.[3] People who combine low H with high X are more likely than others to use sexual innuendo in their speech. They may strike suggestive body language and wear revealing clothes. These behaviours will become less common as the low-H, high-X person gets older, but probably not until the person is beyond the age when they really should have stopped.

Why do low H and high X make for such an exhibitionistic style? Consider first the high-X part of the package: people high in X are socially confident in general, and they see themselves as physically attractive.[4] (This view is at least somewhat justified, because as we note in Chapter 3, high-X people are considered by others to be more attractive, on average, than low-X people are.) Also, high-X people have a rather high sex drive on average, so an overtly sexual style of behaviour comes rather naturally to them.[5] Now consider the low-H part: on average, people low in H don't really have a higher sex drive, nor do other people consider them especially attractive. But low-H people do like to manipulate others, and they're willing to use their physical and social charms to get what they want. And in the context of sexual relationships, what they want can mean two different things: for some low-H people (mainly men), the sex act itself is the ultimate end, and their overt sexuality is a form of hopeful advertising. For other low-H people (mainly women), overt sexuality—and the implied if perhaps insincere promise of sexual receptivity—is a means to other ends, such as the wealth and status they desire and (at least in their own minds) so clearly deserve.[6]

Low H, Low X: The Smug Silent Types

When low levels of Honesty-Humility are combined with *low* levels of eXtraversion, the results are less spectacular but still unpleasant. People who are low in both H and X feel entitled to high status and don't mind exploiting others. Unlike low-H, high-X people, however, they lack the charisma to charm or bully their way into leadership positions. And in fact, although low-H, low-X people want status—in the sense of having the deference and admiration of others—they don't really get much of a thrill from being a leader. Instead, their ideal would be a reclusive life of great wealth and luxury, enjoyed in private behind the high walls of their great estate.

Low-H, low-X people sound like snobs, and that's because they *are* snobs. Sometimes people will mistakenly decide that a *high*-H, low-X person is stuck up, simply because that person is rather aloof, not being much interested in social interaction (see Box 4–2 for a classic fictional case). But when the low-X person is also *low* in H, the perception of haughtiness is accurate. For the low-H, low-X person, it's not just that they prefer to be alone; it's also that other people—apart from a few high-status VIPs—are beneath their concern.

Overall, the low-H, low-X person probably has a lot less capacity to cause problems than does the low-H, high-X person. But this doesn't mean that a low level of X in itself is a good thing, or that a high level of X in itself is a bad thing. Instead, high X tends to amplify the effects of a person's level of H, whether high or low. When a person is low in H, the social confidence and charisma of high X can make that person really dangerous. But when a person is high in H, those same features of high X appear in a much different light: genuine friendliness, modest sexiness, humble leadership. High X people who are low in H are the people you love to hate, but high X people who are high in H are the people you love to like.

BOX 4–2   Pride and Prejudice—and Personality

Among the all-time favourite novels in English literature is Jane Austen's *Pride and Prejudice*, set in rural England of the early 19th century. The heroine of the story, Elizabeth Bennet, eventually falls in love with the rich and handsome Mr. Darcy, but not before her perception of his personality undergoes a profound change.

When Elizabeth first meets the aristocratic Mr. Darcy at a ball, he is aloof and unfriendly, seemingly disdainful of nearly everyone around him, including Elizabeth and her relatives. But after a few more meetings, Mr. Darcy becomes captivated by Elizabeth's spirited and free-thinking personality (in terms of the HEXACO model, she is rather high in both X and O). He proposes marriage to her, and is shocked when she rejects him and bluntly explains her reasons for disliking him—basically, Elizabeth perceives Mr. Darcy to be a low-X, low-A, low-H kind of guy. (On the first two counts, Elizabeth is probably right; he is clearly not very outgoing or cheerful, and by his own admission he is resentful, critical, and unforgiving.) Mr. Darcy then embarks on some soul searching, as he realizes how he is perceived by others.

Elizabeth's view of Mr. Darcy is also influenced by a certain Mr. Wickham, whose own easy charm gives the impression of a high-X, high-H person. Mr. Wickham had spread some rumours that cast doubt on Mr. Darcy's integrity, and these had helped consolidate Elizabeth's "prejudice" against the latter. But after rejecting Mr. Darcy's proposal, Elizabeth learns that it is Mr. Wickham who lacks integrity—he is a devious manipulator, very low in H.

Meanwhile, Elizabeth also learns that Mr. Darcy's personality is, in some respects, very different from what she had believed. For all of his apparent arrogance, Mr. Darcy is actually known for his generosity to the poor and his fairness toward his servants, who can see that he doesn't really have an excess of "pride." Mr. Darcy is high in H after all.

At this point, Elizabeth is horrified to discover that Mr. Wickham has run off with Elizabeth's flirty younger sister, Lydia, whose actions could fatally damage the social standing of the entire family. Mr. Darcy intervenes to rescue the flighty and foolish Lydia—but not as a way of gaining Elizabeth's favour; he tries to keep his actions secret from her. When she inadvertently finds out how Mr. Darcy had saved her sister, Elizabeth fully grasps the error of her earlier rejection of him.

Mr. Darcy had given up any hope of winning Elizabeth's affections, but he later tells Elizabeth that his feelings for her are unchanged and that he still hopes to marry her. She tells him that she now feels the same way for him, and happily accepts his proposal.

In a later conversation, Elizabeth and Mr. Darcy discuss how he first fell in love with her. He had despised the flattery and deference that so many people had shown him on account of his high social status, and he was fascinated by Elizabeth's "impertinence" and "liveliness of mind." As for Elizabeth herself, her thoughts and actions throughout the story suggest a very high level of H. At one point she jokes to her older sister Jane that she first realized her affection for Mr. Darcy when she saw the grounds of his estate, yet in fact Elizabeth had known all along about his wealth and status. But Elizabeth's readiness to criticize suggests that she was not so high in A. In this regard she differs from Jane, who sometimes exasperates Elizabeth through her extraordinary patience and forgivingness.

Elizabeth's initial misperception of Mr. Darcy's level of the H factor raises a more general question: How well do you have to know a person to be able to judge his or her personality? We'll discuss this question in detail in Chapter 5.

Low H, Low A: Just Plain Nasty

People who combine low Honesty-Humility and low Agreeableness are very difficult to get along with. On the one hand, they're inclined to manipulate and exploit you. On the other, they're always getting angry at your attempts (or at least, what they claim to see as your attempts) to exploit them.

Now, some traits belonging to the H factor are unrelated to the A factor, and vice versa. For example, knowing whether a person is sincere—in the sense of not using false ingratiation or flattery in order to get what one wants—tells you basically nothing about whether that person will be even-tempered or patient, stubborn or flexible.

Nevertheless, some traits that are related to H are also related to A, and vice versa. For example, modesty (in the sense of not having a strong sense of superiority or entitlement) is mainly related to H, but it's also somewhat related to A. Conversely, gentleness (in the sense of being lenient rather than harsh in judging others) is mainly related to A, but it's also somewhat related to H. As a result, modesty and gentleness are somewhat correlated with each other, even though they mainly represent different factors.

What this means is that the combination of low H and low A reveals itself in many familiar personality traits. One such trait is aggressiveness: low-H, low-A people are chronically involved in conflicts. Their readiness to offend is matched only by their readiness to take offence. To other people, they seem profoundly hypocritical, always exploiting others in ways that they themselves would never tolerate. In some ways, their litigiousness can work to their advantage: by being low H, they're always ready to take the most advantage of others, and by being low A, they're always ready to stop others from taking the least advantage of them. But the self-ishness and argumentativeness of low-H, low-A people can quickly alienate others, and they can easily end up losing friends and allies. In this way the low-H, low-A person can miss out on opportunities for cooperation with others—cooperation that would ultimately have been more rewarding than perpetual conflict.

Beyond the litigious selfishness described above, the combination of low H and low A shows up in a couple of other unpleasant traits. One of these is vindictiveness or vengefulness: low-H, low-A people get mad, and they love to get even. Now, even low A in isolation (that is, without low H) is associated with a reluctance to forgive others. In fact, having a "forgive and forget" mentality is one of the core traits of high A, and low-A people are very slow to resume cordial relations with someone who has offended them. But when low A is combined with low H, the result is something more than merely an attitude of "once bitten, twice shy." When low-H, low-A people are aggrieved, they want revenge, and they'll take it if given the chance.[7]

One reason for the vindictiveness of low-H, low-A people is that low H can expand one's opportunities for anger. Recall that low-H people think they're entitled to special treatment and that low-A people are intolerant of being treated unfairly. Now, when low-H, low-A people really *are* treated badly, they're outraged: the (genuine) unfairness of the treatment they've received is magnified by their own expectation of being treated with extra respect and consideration. And of course, a person who combines low H with low A will be quite willing to exaggerate their anger, or even to feign it outright, as a calculated tactic for gaining compensation from an (ostensibly) offending party.

In low-H, low-A people, the urge for revenge is unlikely to be kept in check by any ethical restraint. High-H people feel at least some discomfort with the idea of harming others, even when those others aren't so innocent; in contrast, low-H people don't feel the same pangs of moral conscience. This vengefulness will be even stronger when the low-H, low-A person is also low in E: a low level of E means that the person will have less fear of escalating the conflict, and also less empathy or pity for the offending party.

Another feature of the low-H, low-A personality is cynicism: people low in both H and A tend to see the world as a hostile place, full of people who are out to take advantage of them. For the low-H, low-A person, it's better to beat them to the punch: screw them before they screw you. Both elements contribute to this cynicism. People low in A have a hair-trigger sensitivity to being insulted or exploited by others, so they tend to see people as malevolent. But also, people low in H are themselves looking to take advantage of others, and they tend to assume that other people are motivated by the same selfishness and greed. In fact, they tend to see apparently honest people either as closet hypocrites or as naive fools.

Low H, High A: Inoffensive but Insincere

For the most part, the combination of low Honesty-Humility with high Agreeableness is a lot less toxic than the low-H, low-A combination. People who are low in H but high in A are still greedy, sneaky people who are looking out for number one. But because they're much more even-tempered and easygoing, they're a lot easier to get along with. Even though you'll want to be alert to what the low-H, high-A person is up to, you won't be the target of much overt hostility from such a person.

In their style of dealing with other people, persons who are low in H and high in A are different from their low-H, low-A counterparts. For one thing, the low-H, high-A people don't take things so personally. When they're mistreated, they don't get so distracted by the desire for revenge; instead, they let bygones be bygones when this is to their advantage. This willingness to forgive and forget makes them smoother political operators; to paraphrase Lord Palmerston, they have no permanent enemies, just permanent interests. (Of course, they might have no permanent friends either, especially if they're low in E and low in X, but that's fine from their point of view.) Low-H, high-A persons are willing to take advantage of others, yet they're not especially quick to react against those who take advantage of them. It's as if they prefer to keep their options open for future opportunities to cooperate—and exploit.

Another feature of the low-H, high-A personality is the inclination to use ingratiation as a tactic for influencing people. Even though a low-H, *low*-A person can certainly also be ingratiating, it comes even more easily to a person whose low H is blended with *high* A: a high level of A allows one to tolerate people who are rather unlikeable, and even to be very polite to them—high-A people find it easy to hold their nose and their tongue. And of course, a low level of H allows one to deceive people for personal gain—low-H people don't mind being false. So if you have something that the low-H, high-A person wants, you'll be on the receiving end of a lot of flattery and fake friendliness.

BOX 4–3	Personalities of US Presidents of the 1960s and 1970s

In their book *Character, Leadership, and Personality in the White House*, Steven J. Rubenzer and Thomas R. Faschingbauer examined the personalities of US presidents from George Washington to George W. Bush.[8] They contacted over 100 biographers, journalists, and scholars, each of whom was an expert on one or more presidents, and asked those experts to rate the presidents' personalities. The questionnaire that was used for this project was designed to measure the Big Five factors (see Chapter 2), not the HEXACO factors. But this particular questionnaire contains some subscales that allow us to make some reasonable estimates about the presidents' levels of the HEXACO personality dimensions.[9]

Many of the results obtained by Rubenzer and Faschingbauer in their expert survey are interesting. Some particularly sharp contrasts are evident among the presidents of the 1960s and 1970s. Collectively, these presidents showed several distinct combinations of the H and A factors, while also differing in several other dimensions. Below are some highlights that we have summarized based on the findings reported by Rubenzer and Faschingbauer.

John F. Kennedy was somewhat low in H but higher in A. He had little difficulty manipulating and deceiving others. A big spender during his days in the House of Representatives, he would often borrow money from his staff members without repaying them. As noted by historian Paul Johnson, Kennedy cultivated the reputation of a thinker by publishing several scholarly works, but these were actually ghostwritten for him by others.[10] But despite being low in H, Kennedy was not low in A: experts indicated that he wasn't defensive, fault finding, harsh, or unforgiving.

Lyndon Johnson was very low in both H and A. Of all the presidents, it was perhaps Johnson who had the lowest level of H. In his early years, he was obsequious toward those in authority, and in public office he continued to use flattery to influence people, along with outright lying. He saw himself as superior to others and was particularly vain about his personal appearance. A former high school teacher, Johnson hired some of his ex-students to work for him in Washington—and then kept for himself a large fraction of their salaries. In addition to these various indications of low H, Johnson exhibited the signs of low A. Crude and vulgar, he had an explosive temper and often yelled abusively at his subordinates. More generally, he was an extremely critical, fault-finding boss who was nonetheless highly defensive about his own shortcomings and unforgiving of those who offended him.

Richard Nixon rivals Johnson as an extremely low-H, low-A president. Nixon's pattern of dishonest behaviour ran throughout his life in politics, most infamously during the Watergate Scandal, which erupted after he arranged for illegal wiretaps of his political opponents and then attempted to hide that he had done so. Eisenhower chose Nixon as his vice-presidential running mate in 1952, yet Eisenhower distrusted him, in part because of a questionable scheme whereby Nixon had received gifts from political supporters. Years before then, Nixon's scheming and treachery had earned him the nickname Tricky Dick. And Nixon's deceitfulness was matched by his hostility. As revealed by the White House tapes (he bugged his own Oval Office), he was deeply suspicious and unforgiving of others, full of bitterness and resentment. He was obsessed with real and perceived opponents, many of whom he included on his famous enemies list.

Gerald Ford was relatively high in both H and A. He was respected by political allies and opponents alike for his integrity and modesty. Martha Griffiths, one of his opponents in the House of Representatives, said that in all her years in the House, she never heard Ford make a statement that was even partly false. An unpretentious man, he was respectful toward his staff; on one occasion, when Ford's dog had soiled a carpet, he insisted on cleaning up the mess himself rather than letting a staff member do so. Also high in A, Ford was known as an even-tempered man who felt little hostility or resentment.

Jimmy Carter was relatively high in H but somewhat lower in A. Like Ford, he was known as an ethical president. He had high moral standards, as expressed in an unwillingness to manipulate others or to stretch the truth, and was seen as modest and unassuming. With regard to the A factor, Carter was probably somewhat lower: one biographer made repeated references to Carter's "famous temper," highlighting several occasions when he reacted angrily.[11]

The results reported by Rubenzer and Faschingbauer suggest that these presidents also differed in several other dimensions. For example, Kennedy and Carter were both high in O, whereas Johnson, Nixon, and Ford were low. Nixon was very low in X, whereas Kennedy, Johnson, and Ford were very high, with Carter in between. Kennedy was lower in C than were the other presidents in this group. But the differences among them in the H and A factors are probably the most striking of all.

Low H, Low C: An Employer's Worst Nightmare

People who combine low Honesty-Humility with low Conscientiousness are the last people you'd want to hire. Surveys of employers indicate that the most desirable traits in employees are dependability, reliability, and responsibility. These traits combine high H and high C, so workers who are low in both these dimensions will be pretty much the opposite of what any boss would want. Imagine the kind of employee who not only has a natural tendency to be sloppy and lazy, but also has no work *ethic*—no sense of any moral obligation to give a fair day's work for a fair day's pay. It doesn't bother their conscience to be late for work or even to skip work entirely. It doesn't bother their conscience if they get little work done or if the work is shoddy. Even if they're treated well by their employer and their co-workers, they won't have much sense of responsibility or loyalty to them. And this extends beyond simply being an unreliable worker. The low-H, low-C employee is the one who is most likely to steal money or merchandise from the workplace.[12]

The delinquent tendencies of low-H, low-C persons aren't confined to the workplace. People who have both the exploitiveness of low H and the impulsiveness of low C are doubly inclined toward criminal behaviour in general. On the one hand, they're strongly tempted to take what they want from others, whether by force or by fraud; they're looking out for number one. On the other, they lack the self-control to inhibit these urges even when they'd be better off—from their own selfish perspective—to keep their impulses in check.

This blend of low H and low C is in large part responsible for the characteristic that forensic psychologists call "psychopathy"— the tendency to commit immoral and antisocial acts without remorse. Researchers in this area have identified four related aspects of psychopathy: (1) a manipulative, "conning" style of interaction with others; (2) an erratic, uncontrolled, impulsive lifestyle; (3) a callous insensitivity to others' concerns; and (4) a pattern of chronic and varied criminal activity.[13] Each of these tendencies is related to low levels of H and of C, as well as to low levels of E: manipulation is mainly low H, "erratic" impulsivity is mainly low C, callousness is mainly low E, and antisocial behaviour (which is more a consequence of personality traits than a personality trait in its own right) is related to all three.[14]

Some sociologists have attempted to explain criminal tendencies with a "general theory of crime" that takes personality characteristics into account.[15] But this theory captures only half the story, as it focuses on the traits that define low C, omitting any role for the traits that define low H. According to the theory, everyone is about equally tempted to exploit others; it's just that some people lack the self-control to inhibit their selfish impulses. But make no mistake: people differ greatly in the inclination to exploit other people—the H factor does exist, and it's crucial for understanding criminality.[16]

People with the blend of low H and low C can also hurt others without committing any crimes. Low-H, low-C people have a double inclination to cheat on their spouses: persons low in H won't feel much moral obligation to be sexually faithful to their partner, and persons low in C won't exert much control over their sexual impulses, even when common sense would recommend it. Once again, other personality factors would likely also come into play. A low level of E will make this combination even worse, through having a weaker sense of emotional attachment and empathy for one's spouse.[17]

This same combination of selfishness and poor impulse control also means that low-H, low-C people are likely vectors for sexually transmitted diseases: they won't be too fastidious about whom they have sex with[18] or about having safe sex, and they'll be far too interested in their own gratification to be concerned about the health of their partners.

In addition, low-H, low-C persons are prime candidates for problem gambling: the prospect of winning big money is very attractive to them, and they just don't know when to quit (or maybe they do know, but they still don't quit).[19] Now, problem gambling is often viewed as an addiction, similar to alcoholism or to dependence on various drugs. And just as people who are low in both H and C are at risk for gambling problems, they're also at risk for substance abuse problems. As we've noted, low C is associated with a lack of self-control, and when this is combined with low H, there is not much sense of moral wrongdoing associated with drug or alcohol abuse. (In contrast, a *high*-H, low-C person might be at least somewhat deterred from drug and alcohol addiction by the sense that they are letting down the people around them.)

Low H, High C: Selfish Ambition

In some ways, a high level of Conscientiousness can mitigate the effects of a low level of Honesty-Humility. People who combine low H with high C are still selfish at heart, but they can control their impulses. They can think in terms of their long-run interests, so they tend to behave responsibly. And because they like rules and order, they're less inclined to break laws, even though they're perfectly willing to exploit other people.

The challenge for low-H, high-C people is to satisfy their desire for wealth and status while maintaining an orderly, predictable style of life. These are the kinds of people who like to find legal technicalities they can exploit to their best advantage. (They would rather not cheat on their taxes, but if they can find a loophole to avoid paying, that's great.) For the low-H, high-C person, the spirit of the law is unimportant if the letter of the law allows them a way to profit.

People who combine low H and high C are willing to work hard and strive for high goals. But their need for achievement is focused on personal gain and glory; they don't really care whether their ambition is ultimately for the good or ill of other people. By contrast, people who are high in both C and H will focus their effort only on projects that are ethically sound, not just on whatever will bring them money and prestige.

Low-H, high-C people are generally much better workers than low-H, low-C people—the former will at least show up and do some real work. But it's still important to keep a close eye on them. Low-H, high-C people will be ambitious climbers of the company ladder, but they're ultimately concerned only about themselves. As long as their interests coincide with those of the organization and its people, there's no problem. But if those interests should someday diverge, they won't be constrained by any feelings of genuine loyalty. Their high level of C means they have a conscience in the sense of achieving goals and maintaining order, yet their low level of H means they lack a conscience in the sense of being fair and ethical.

As noted earlier, low-H, high-C people appreciate structure and order and generally stay within the rules. But for high-C people who have an extremely low level of H, the desire for wealth and power—along with their sense of entitlement and their taste for deception—can be strong enough to override any preference for abiding by the law. These people are prone to white-collar crimes such as embezzlement, tax evasion, investment fraud, insurance fraud, and bribery.[20] If they can find a way to commit such crimes with low risk of getting caught, they may well take advantage of it. One especially attractive scenario would be to attain some high-ranking position—in business, in government, or elsewhere—that would provide the chance to commit fraud on a repeated, ongoing basis, operating under the radar of anyone who might detect them.

All of this raises an interesting question: Which kind of criminal is more harmful to society? Is it the low-H, low-C common criminal or the low-H, high-C white-collar criminal? It's probable that overall, a lot more harm is done by low-H, low-C persons, insofar as they are so much more likely to commit crimes. But on a per-criminal basis, low-H, high-C people who commit crimes are probably more effective and more successful—and potentially more harmful—than their less disciplined and less careful counterparts who blend low H and low C.[21]

We should mention one other characteristic—unrelated to C—that can contribute to the possibility that low-H people will successfully exploit others. A low-H person who is very smart—in the classic sense of having good reasoning skills of the kind measured by IQ tests—is much more likely to rise to a position of high status, whether in business or finance or politics or the professions or academia. Having attained a lofty position, the low-H person has all the more opportunity to act on his or her sense of entitlement and on the urge to exploit others for personal gain. Think of the Wall Street "quants" whose financial innovations brought them huge riches but also helped bring the US economy to the brink of disaster in 2008.

BOX 4–4	Personality and the Stanford Prison Experiment

As we've explained, people who combine low H and low C are the classic common criminals. In contrast, people who combine low H with high C usually inhibit their inclination to exploit other people and are much less likely to commit crimes; in fact, a moderately low-H person who has anything more than a very low level of C will probably control any criminal impulses well enough. But what happens when such a person simply sees no need to restrain the urge to take advantage of others?

Some evidence on this point comes from the famous Stanford prison experiment of Philip Zimbardo.[22] The 24 men who participated in the experiment in 1971 were all college students recruited through advertisements that requested volunteers for "a psychological study of prison life." All participants selected for the experiment were screened for any history of antisocial behaviour. Each was randomly assigned to one of two roles—prison guard or prisoner—and placed in a simulated prison in the basement of a Stanford University psychology building. The "prison guards" were given a whistle and a police nightstick and dressed in a khaki-coloured uniform; the "prisoners" were chained around the ankles and dressed in a plain smock with no underwear. The prison guards were told they had power over the prisoners and that they could use it to maintain order within the prison as long as no physical harm was done to the prisoners.

What happened next was remarkable. The prison guards almost immediately began to abuse their power, punishing the prisoners harshly and arbitrarily. They confiscated mattresses and did not empty sanitary buckets, leaving the jail cells extremely unpleasant. To punish a rebellion by some of the prisoners, the guards stripped some prisoners naked and locked others in an extremely small and completely dark closet. The mistreatment of the prisoners continued for six days, when Zimbardo finally suspended the experiment in order to avoid traumatizing the participants. He concluded that "good" people (here, seemingly ordinary college students) can do unthinkably "bad" things when placed in situation where they are led to believe they have legitimate power to do so. Zimbardo suggested that it's as if each of us contains both a Dr. Jekyll and a Mr. Hyde, with the situation determining which identity will come out.[23]

Although situational pressures do have a strong influence on behaviour, the results of a recent study suggest some role for personality in explaining what happened during the Stanford prison experiment.[24] According to the findings of Thomas Carnahan and Samuel McFarland, the particularly nasty behaviours shown by the students might not have been due entirely to the prison guard role that was assigned to them. Instead, the students who responded to the prison study ad might have had some characteristics that predisposed them to mistreat other people when placed in a context that facilitated rather than discouraged such behaviour.

To examine this possibility, Carnahan and McFarland recruited some research participants using two advertisements. One of these was essentially identical to the one that Zimbardo had used, introducing the study as "a psychological study of *prison life*." The other introduced it simply as "a psychological study." The researchers then compared the volunteers who were recruited via the two different ads, measuring them on several personality variables. The results indicated that participants who responded to the "prison" advertisement showed much higher scores on personality scales related to low H and low A than did participants who responded to the generic ad. These results suggest that the participants of the Stanford prison experiment might have been below average in their levels of H and A and that the shocking results of that experiment might have been less extreme had most of the participants been average or higher in these personality traits.

But if the students of the Stanford prison experiment were low in H and A, why did they only begin acting like tyrants when placed in the prison simulation? How is it that they were otherwise normal college students without any history of antisocial behaviour? We think the likely reason involves the C factor: presumably, these college students without any history of serious antisocial behaviour were (at a minimum) not particularly low in C-related traits such as self-control and self-discipline. Under normal circumstances—when the "rules" forbid the abuse of others and when the consequences for breaking rules are predictable and unpleasant—these traits inhibit such behaviour. But in a situation where the rules have changed or no longer apply, the "braking" effect of C on criminal behaviour is removed, and a person who is low in H (or worse still, low in H *and* A *and* E) is much more likely to mistreat other people.

The Stanford prison experiment involved a situation that "liberated" bad intentions from the restraint of self-control, but it isn't hard to imagine others. Think of wartime atrocities committed by soldiers who had been law-abiding citizens in their home countries. Think of the abuses inflicted by officials of authoritarian regimes against dissenting citizens. Think of the outbreaks of looting seen in the wake of some natural disasters (or even some sporting events). Without the rule of law, the C factor won't necessarily counteract the effects of low H.

Low H, Low O: Shallow and Narrow

The word that best describes people who blend low Honesty-Humility with low Openness to Experience is "shallow." Or perhaps it's "superficial." Low-H, low-O people are interested in money and status and not much else. For these people, science is worthwhile only as a source of marketable technology, nature is appreciated only for raw materials and real estate, and art is interesting only as an investment or a trophy. For these people, to contemplate the meaning of life or the human condition is to waste time that could be spent acquiring new toys and showing them off.

Low-H, low-O people who strike it rich can be almost breathtakingly tacky in flaunting their wealth. Their urge to make ostentatious displays is unconstrained by any aesthetic taste or sense of harmony with nature. These people would want to have the biggest mansion in the neighbourhood, regardless of how many old trees must be cut down or how much it destroys the balance of the surroundings.[25]

Low-H, low-O people judge others mainly on the basis of their wealth and prestige. Such people have particularly little respect for those whose accomplishments are of the kind associated with high O. Their attitude toward (say) an accomplished scientist or learned scholar is simply, "If you're so smart, why aren't you rich?" Likewise, people who blend low H and low O are baffled by those who, having the opposite combination of traits, simply don't care about keeping up with the Joneses. The idea of deliberately choosing a smaller car or a smaller house—of living a minimalist lifestyle more generally—strikes them as utter folly.

The blend of low H and low O also comes with a particular set of attitudes about how others are to be treated. Low-H people are inclined to exploit others, and low-O people find it hard to relate to those whose backgrounds are different from their own. When low H and low O are combined, the result is a person who is especially ready to take advantage of those who seem different or strange or alien. Now, low-H, low-O people might feel some discomfort about being too ruthless in taking advantage of people who look and talk and think like they do. After all, the community has certain standards about how things are done, and one doesn't want to look bad. But when it comes to those far away, or those too different to identify with, or those not protected by community norms, there is no holding back. Moral considerations don't apply to outsiders.

This attitude is evident in the kinds of business or investment decisions favoured by low-H, low-O people. For them, the bottom line is the bottom line, and "ethical investing" is for suckers and weirdos: if there's money to be made, there's no point in worrying about anything so abstract as the environment or human rights.[26]

You might guess that the low-H, low-O blend has certain implications for political attitudes. And you'd be right. We'll discuss these implications in depth in Chapter 7.

Low H, High O: Sophisticated Snobbery

The combination of low Honesty-Humility and high Openness to Experience has some very unpleasant features, but these are much different from those of the low-H, low-O combination.

People who blend low H with high O are still inclined to show off, but they generally do so with some artistic flair. At the extremes—when they have enough money to spend—the result is likely to be aesthetically impressive but morally offensive. Think of the palace at Versailles, or the Taj Mahal. (We mean the original Taj Mahal, not the Atlantic City hotel casino; the latter is probably a better example of low H and *low* O.)

A more common expression of low H and high O is snobbery of an artistic or intellectual kind. People low in H and high in O love to show how cultured and learned they are. They enjoy putting big words together, especially when those big words are currently becoming stylish; it doesn't matter so much whether the long string of big words actually makes much sense. You could say that their hermeneutic discourse is informed by the extant paradigms of pedagogy and governance, or something like that. We suspect that intellectual movements such as postmodernism hold a special attraction for low-H, high-O people.[27]

For low-H, high-O people, the arts are partly an expression of the human condition, but partly just a vehicle for showing off their originality. They wear their artistic talent like a badge, often flaunting it as a way of establishing their superiority. And particularly where male artists are concerned, that talent is deployed as a tool for seducing impressionable women (or, depending on their tastes, for seducing impressionable men).

People who are low in H and high in O are aggressively nonconformist. Their high O results in a natural inclination to be unconventional; their low H in a lack of consideration for other people. The result is a person who takes a special joy in offending community standards and who defies conventional morality partly in order to gain a reputation for being radical. Especially when low C is also involved, such people like to live as very public libertines, openly indulging their tastes for sex and drugs. And when they direct a movie or write a book or create a piece of art, those works are often calculated to be as offensive and obscene as possible. Low-H, high-O people are rebellious, but they are rebels without a conscience, motivated mainly by self-gratification and by the status that their provocativeness gains them in the eyes of at least some people.

BOX 4–5 A Tale of Two Art Collectors

Hermann Wilhelm Göring was a powerful figure in Nazi Germany; indeed, he was Adolf Hitler's handpicked successor. In 1946 he was convicted at the Nuremberg trials of waging aggressive war, of war crimes, and of crimes against humanity. Sentenced to death, he committed suicide the day before his scheduled execution.

Göring was most notorious for the crimes for which he was convicted at Nuremberg, but he also displayed a variety of common low-H characteristics. He was thoroughly corrupt, using his power as Hitler's deputy to accumulate personal wealth. He did so by seizing the property of Jews and by taking bribes from others who wanted Jewish property for themselves.

Like many other low-H people, Göring enjoyed an extravagant lifestyle. He drove a Mercedes 540Ks, one of only 32 ever made, and he lived in a sprawling hunting lodge he built on a vast forest estate outside Berlin. When he married a famous opera star (his second wife), the wedding was no less grandiose than a royal wedding, and featured Hitler as the best man. Göring wore garish jewellery and extravagant uniforms and suits, which he changed several times a day.

Some of Göring's characteristics suggest that he combined a low level of H with a high level of O. First, his choice of clothing was eccentric and flamboyant: many people would remember him wearing costumes that resembled medieval hunting garb or Roman togas. According to the Italian foreign minister of the time, one of Göring's fur coats looked like "what a high-end prostitute wears to the opera." His fashion sense was not always received well by others, but it clearly stood out. Second, he had a wide range of interests, something that he was rather boastful of; he once described himself as "the last Renaissance man." He enjoyed opera, and even before his Nazi days he was an avid collector of art. During the Second World War, he amassed the greatest private art collection of the time by systematically looting museums all over occupied Europe as well as Jewish collections. He also created a private gallery on his estate, filling it with 2,000 priceless paintings he had stolen. Göring's predation of Europe's art treasures reveals his low-H personality, but his considerable efforts in creating his own private gallery suggest that he had some genuine intrinsic interests in fine art—even though his artistic taste seems to have been weak at best.

Dennis Kozlowski, former CEO of Tyco International, was born one month after Göring's suicide. Kozlowski became a rising star in the U.S. business world, building Tyco into a giant global conglomerate. His luck began to fail, however, with a charge of sales tax evasion relating to a $13.1 million purchase of art (see below), which led to a prosecution involving much larger felony charges. Kozlowski was later convicted of misappropriating millions of dollars of Tyco funds.

Unlike Göring, Kozlowski was no war criminal. But like Göring, he enjoyed a lavish lifestyle and collected some very expensive works of art. He lived in an $18 million apartment in New York City, which he filled with luxury items that showed his expensive but (one might say) rather unrefined tastes. In this residence, the prosecutors found such extravagances as a $6,000 shower curtain and a $15,000 dog-shaped umbrella stand. Kozlowski famously threw a $2 million party for his wife's 40th birthday. The guests at the party could admire an ice sculpture of Michelangelo's *David*, which "urinated" vodka into their glasses.

Besides the tacky items mentioned above, the apartment also displayed some famous works of art, including paintings by Renoir and Monet. But the way that Kozlowski bought these paintings suggests that he may not have been motivated by a high-O appreciation of art. According to the testimony of the art dealer who arranged the purchase of the paintings, Kozlowski wanted to buy works painted by "high-end names"; on one occasion, he bought four such paintings, including a Renoir for $8.8 million, within an hour. One may wonder whether these paintings were purchased solely as trophies, functionally not much different from the shower curtain, the dog-shaped umbrella stand, and the vodka-dispensing statue of David. The method of purchasing these items suggests to us a low rather than a high level of O.

By the way, don't misunderstand these examples as suggesting that all art collectors are low in H. Many people who collect art are very ethical persons who have no interest in ostentatious display.

This completes our short field guide to the many varieties of low-H people. In the next chapter, we'll turn to the question of how accurately people can judge one another's personalities—especially the H factor.

5

CAN YOU TELL SOMEONE'S LEVEL OF H?

Think of a casual acquaintance of yours and try to imagine what that person would or wouldn't do. Cheat on their taxes? Keep the money found in a wallet? Manipulate the boss to get a promotion? Use other people to climb the social ladder? In this chapter, we're interested in the question of how accurately you can estimate another person's level of the H factor. Can you tell at first sight whether a person is high or low in H? Or can you never tell, even after knowing them for many years?

Personality in Strangers

Let's start with strangers. Researchers have tried to find out whether people can judge the personalities of people they've just met. In these research studies, participants are asked to rate a stranger's personality after just a few minutes of observation—perhaps after a short conversation, or watching the person in a short (and silent) video clip.

The results of these studies indicate that people are at least somewhat accurate when it comes to judging strangers' personality traits, at least for traits associated with the X factor. Apparently, it's fairly easy to judge how outgoing or lively a person is, even on first encounter. For the other personality factors, including the H factor, you generally can't judge people accurately when you first meet them.

BOX 5-1 Narcissism at First Sight

Although people generally can't tell another person's level of H upon first meeting, the results of one study suggest that the combination of low H and high X is at least somewhat apparent even to strangers. As we discussed in Chapter 4, people who combine low H with high X are narcissistic. They have a grandiose sense of self-worth and a strong sense of being entitled to others' admiration and attention. Narcissistic people tend to brag about their achievements and to flaunt their assets (whether financial or physical or otherwise), and they generally convey the attitude that they're better than you are.

One study examined whether people can tell how narcissistic someone is just by looking at a photograph of that person.[1] In this study, the photographed people didn't know that their pictures would be taken, so the images in the photos probably showed their typical appearance. Those photographed people had completed a self-report narcissism scale, and their scores varied widely, ranging from very self-effacing to very self-promoting. When university students were asked to estimate the narcissism levels of all the photographed persons—all of whom were strangers to the students—their ratings were more accurate than chance, with correlations in the .20s.

How were people able to judge the narcissism levels of the photographed persons? In part, they noted whether the stranger was wearing flashy, expensive clothing. Also, in the case of a female stranger, narcissism was attributed (usually correctly) to those who showed cleavage, who wore heavy makeup, and who plucked their eyebrows. Still, the level of accuracy wasn't high enough to be of much practical value; you wouldn't want to rely much on these clues if you were trying to judge people's levels of H—for example, in choosing an investment manager or finding a blind date for a friend. Also, these results apply to people who combine low H with *high* X; it would be harder to identify low-H people who are also *low* in X (see Chapter 4), because their low-H clues would be much less prominently displayed.

But can you *ever* get an accurate idea of someone's level of H? Or is the H factor such a subtle aspect of personality that you can never really judge people's levels very accurately even after many interactions with them? We'll discuss this shortly, but first a more basic question: How can we figure out whether you're accurate or not?

One way to evaluate your accuracy involves the use of personality questionnaires—or, as they are usually called, personality *inventories*. Many personality inventories have both a "self-report" form—in which a person responds to statements about his or her own personality—and also an "observer report" form—in which a person responds to statements about some other person's personality. (See the Appendix for the self-report and observer report forms of the short HEXACO Personality Inventory.) By comparing your observer report about a person's level of the H factor with that person's own self-report, we could likely get a good sense of your accuracy.

Self-Reports of H: Are They Honest?

A little later in this chapter, we'll give some results indicating how accurately people can judge another person's level of the H factor. But first, you might wonder whether it makes sense to use a person's self-report to decide how accurately you've judged his or her level of H. Indeed, people sometimes tell us it is impossible to measure the H factor through any kind of self-report inventory. The problem, they suggest, is that dishonest people won't admit to being dishonest, because their very dishonesty causes them to claim falsely that they are honest. Superficially, this is logical, but the argument is based on a misunderstanding of what the H factor is all about: low-H people are willing to deceive for personal gain, but this doesn't mean they're pathologically unable or unwilling to tell the truth. When responding to personality inventories in anonymous research settings, low-H persons don't have any incentive to lie about themselves. In fact, like other people, they generally find it more satisfying (and a lot easier) simply to describe themselves frankly and accurately. In such settings, low-H people are generally quite willing to indicate that they would act in low-H ways, such as cheating or manipulating others to get ahead. Therefore, self-reports of H are likely to be very accurate, at least when these are provided in anonymous research settings.

This is evident when we look at people's scores on self-report scales measuring the H factor. Just as we find for the other five factors, a few people have very high scores, a few people have very low scores, and most people are in between. If low-H people were simply "faking" to present themselves as high in H, we'd expect most people to be "piled up" at the high end of the scale. Also, most of the people who have high self-reported levels of H *don't* claim to have high levels of other desirable characteristics. If those people were simply faking, they'd likely be presenting themselves as all-around wonderful people.[2]

BOX 5-2
Measuring Personality: Self-Reports (and Observer Reports) Work Better Than You'd Think

To many people, the idea of using questionnaires or inventories to measure personality—or anything else—seems unscientific. In other branches of science, researchers use instruments that measure variables more objectively. For example, when meteorologists measure temperature or humidity or wind speed, they use thermometers and hygrometers and anemometers. They don't ask people how warm or humid or windy it is.

But personality traits are different from the phenomena studied in other sciences. For one thing, a personality trait is a *disposition*—a tendency to show a certain style of behaving and thinking and feeling, as shown across a variety of relevant situations and over a long period of time. So if we want to measure someone's level of a personality trait, we have to capture that disposition—that *tendency*—and there is no physical instrument that can do this. Although researchers have tried various ways of measuring personality (including direct observations of behaviour in controlled settings), the results indicate that well-constructed personality inventories have the crucial advantage of providing accurate personality descriptions with relatively little time and expense. ("Well constructed" is a key phrase here, because many inventories don't measure personality accurately.) We can assess someone's personality in broad outline by getting responses from that person (or from someone who knows him or her well) to a few dozen statements that are carefully developed to tap the traits of interest.

But how do we know that personality inventories are actually accurate? Consider several lines of evidence. First of all, scores on well-designed personality inventories are correlated with other variables that ought to reflect (at least to some extent) people's personalities. For example, when we administer self-report personality inventories to university students, we find that their scores on the C factor predict their grade-point average, that their scores on the O factor predict their level of verbal ability, and that their scores on the X factor predict their popularity with their peers.[3] Moreover, people's scores on personality scales can even predict, to a modest extent, important life outcomes such as mortality/ longevity, occupational attainment, and divorce—even when the personality measurements were made long before these outcomes actually happened.[4]

Another indication that personality inventories are accurate is that there is generally rather close agreement among various observer reports, as made independently by persons who are closely acquainted with the "target" person. In studies of university students' personalities, there is fairly close agreement between the observer reports from their old "hometown" friends, from their new "university" friends, and from their parents—and all of these observer reports correlate rather well with the students' own self-reports. The agreement among observer reports is particularly impressive given that in some cases, the hometown friends and the college friends have never even met one another and have known the target person during different time periods and in different social settings.[5]

All of these findings indicate that personality inventories can provide accurate information. However, none of this is to say that personality inventories will work well under all conditions. In particular, we'd be cautious about using self-reports with people who have an incentive to make a certain impression—imagine, for example, a person providing self-reports in applying for a desirable job or for early parole. Many studies have shown clearly that when people are instructed to "fake good" or "fake bad" on a personality inventory, they can do so.[6] But when people respond to personality inventories in anonymous research settings, nearly all of them describe themselves frankly.

Knowing Someone's Personality: H Is among the Last Things You Learn

Over the years, we've obtained self-reports and observer reports on the HEXACO factors from over 1300 pairs of university students. Some of these pairs were boyfriend and girlfriend, and a few of the pairs were relatives (usually siblings), but most of the pairs were friends, usually of the same sex and often living in the same house. When participating in our research studies, each member of a pair provides self-reports and observer reports in our research labs, without having any chance to consult with the other member.

What we've found is that, on average, self-report levels of H aren't any higher than observer report levels. Our university students don't claim to be any more sincere or modest than their friends say they are. (Note, by the way, that if the students were faking to appear high in H, their self-reports would be much higher than the observer reports from their friends.) And for the most part, if a student has a high self-reported level of H, then his or her friend's observer report is high also; likewise, if a student has a low self-reported level of H, the friend's observer report is probably low too. For these closely acquainted pairs of students, the correlations between self-reports and observer reports on the six HEXACO personality factors are all around .50. (For an explanation of what correlations mean, see Box 2–1.) This is a fairly high level of agreement, and it applies to all six factors, including H.

When we found that there was such good agreement between self-reports and observer reports of personality, we began to wonder: How long do you need to know someone—and how well do you need to know that person—before you can judge their personality? We checked to find out whether the level of agreement was higher for friends who had known each other for a longer time. The results surprised us: the agreement between self-reports and observer reports didn't depend on how long the friends had known each other. In fact, the correlations between self-reports and observer reports were as high for pairs who had known each other for only about one year as they were for pairs who had known each other for several years. This was true for all six HEXACO factors, which suggests that people can get a fairly good idea of one another's levels of H—how sincere or modest they are—within a year.

But even if it doesn't take a long time to learn someone's level of the H factor, it does take a lot of observation: you have to get to know that person rather well. We had also asked the members of each pair of students to indicate how well they knew each other, using a scale from 0 (not at all) to 10 (extremely well). For most pairs, the level of acquaintanceship was very high, generally between 7 and 10; however, a little more than 10% of our participants indicated levels of 6 or below.

We asked for these ratings in order to tell whether the level of agreement between self-reports and observer reports depends on how well people know each other. It does: the correlations between self- and observer reports are generally higher for people who consider themselves to be more closely acquainted.

This result probably doesn't surprise you, but what's interesting is that it doesn't apply for every personality factor. Even when the pairs of students know each other only moderately well—that is, when their ratings are 6 or less—they are able to judge each other's levels of X and E fairly accurately. But this result makes sense in light of some other facts. Apparently, as we noted earlier, you can judge X with at least some accuracy even in strangers,[7] and E shows some fairly large differences between men and women, which means that a person's sex gives at least a rough clue as to their level of the E factor. People can usually make good judgments about X and E even for people whom they know only moderately well.

What's also interesting is that among people who *aren't* very well acquainted, observer reports are noticeably less accurate for

H (and also for A and C, to a lesser degree) than for the other personality factors. When you don't know a person well, you may have a pretty accurate idea of his or her levels for the E, X, and O factors, but you're likely to be less accurate for A, C, and especially H . However, this accuracy appears to increase sharply as people get to know each other better. When we spend a lot of time with a person in a wide variety of contexts, so that we get to know that person well, we can develop a pretty good idea of his or her level of the H factor.[8]

Of course, the results described above reflect an average across many pairs of people: some persons' levels of H are more easily observed, and other persons' levels are less easily observed. Likewise, some persons are better than average at judging someone's H level, some persons worse. (We're quite sure that you, for example, are much better than average.) But until you've had many opportunities to observe a person in widely varied settings or situations, it's better to be cautious in judging their level of H, even if you've known them for many years.

H in the Workplace: Hard to Tell

One implication of these results is that some kinds of relationships probably don't give us enough information to judge other people's levels of the H factor. Consider the workplace. In Western countries, most people interact with their co-workers only when doing the job itself and rarely in other, more private settings. These situations are much less varied than the ones that we share with our friends and spouses and relatives. Moreover, people usually want to make a certain impression on their co-workers—whether supervisors or peers or subordinates—so they're more likely to behave in ways that don't necessarily reveal all aspects of their personalities.

We saw this first-hand when Joshua Bourdage, one of our graduate students, collected personality data from pairs of administrative employees at the university. He was interested in examining how employees try to manage the way they're seen by their co-workers—in other words, their "workplace impression management." Workplace impression management includes behaviours such as self-promotion (e.g., boasting about your experience or education), ingratiation (e.g., flattering your colleagues so that they will like you), exemplification (e.g., pretending to be busy even when you aren't), supplication (e.g., pretending not to understand something in order to get someone's help), and intimidation (e.g., letting others know that you can make things difficult for them).[9] The common feature of these behaviours is that people use them to manipulate their co-workers and supervisors.

We recruited pairs of employees who had worked in the same department for at least six months. The participating employees came to our lab to give self-reports and observer reports on some scales measuring workplace impression management and also on our personality inventory, the HEXACO–PI–R. Each employee gave his or her reports anonymously and confidentially, and independently of his or her co-worker—the same procedure that we used with our pairs of university students, as described above. In this way, we could see whether the employees could tell how much their co-workers were managing impressions at work.

We collected personality reports from about 100 employees. When we first analyzed the data, the results looked very strange:

the employees' self-reports of workplace impression management were almost uncorrelated with the observer reports from their co-workers. It seemed to us that this couldn't be right; surely the co-workers would notice each other's impression management with at least some accuracy. But we checked the data set in several ways, and everything was done correctly. Contrary to what we had expected, there just wasn't much agreement between employees' self-reports and their co-workers' observer reports. And these co-workers had generally known each other for some time—more than 18 months in the typical case—which meant that many of them had had ample opportunity to observe their co-workers.

Now, you might wonder whether the employees were really being frank about how much impression management they were doing in their workplace. If employees generally deny these behaviours, naturally this will result low correlations with the co-workers' reports, if it's the co-workers who are telling us how the employees *really* behave. But this apparently isn't the case: the employees' self-reports indicated just as much impression management, on average, as their co-workers' observer reports did. (And because the responses were given in an anonymous, confidential setting, the employees had no reason to conceal these behaviours.) Apparently, some employees overestimate how much impression management their co-workers do, and other employees underestimate it. These findings mean that you can't always tell what's behind the outward behaviour of your co-workers. Some of those who behave as very good citizens may truly be acting out of good will; others may just be acting.

Not surprisingly, workers who did a lot of impression management tended to be low in the H factor. And our findings for the H factor were similar to those for impression management: employees' self-reports on the H factor were only very weakly correlated with their co-workers' observer reports. Just as co-workers couldn't accurately judge each other's levels of workplace impression management, they also couldn't accurately judge each other's levels of H. Now, the levels of agreement for the other personality factors (except X) were generally somewhat lower in the co-worker sample than in the student sample that we discussed above. As we speculated earlier, these differences probably reflected the fact that the co-workers typically weren't so closely acquainted with each other as were the students (who, as you'll recall, were usually close friends). But what's striking is that the H factor showed particularly low accuracy in the co-worker sample. As we mentioned above, the correlation between self-reports and observer reports was about .50 in our student sample, yet in our co-worker sample it was only about .10.

Why is it difficult to judge accurately the levels of H of your co-workers? It may be because everyday interactions in the workplace don't give many valid clues about people's levels of the H factor. Most workplaces don't offer many situations that let you see plainly which people are high in H and which people are low. Another reason is that people tend not to reveal their levels of H in the workplace: many low-H people make a calculated effort to come across as upstanding employees, but few high-H people do so, which makes it very hard to tell which people are which. (By contrast, people are less willing or less able to manage their impressions *all* of the time, so their friends and spouses and relatives will generally get a pretty good idea of their level of H.) Anyhow, the results of our research suggest that it would be easy to trust co-workers too much—or even to trust them too little—based on the limited information you typically get in the workplace.

To sum up, people are pretty accurate in judging the personalities of those who are close to them—the persons they know well. And for many aspects of personality, people can still make accurate judgments even for people they don't know so well—such as their more distant social acquaintances, or their co-workers. But apparently, this doesn't apply to the H factor: to be really accurate in judging a person's level of H, you usually need to know that person very well.

6

DO HIGH-H PEOPLE FLOCK TOGETHER?

Think of your spouse and your best friends. For any one of these people, you can probably think of some similarities and some differences between his or her personality and yours. But are there some personality traits that you have in common with most—or even all—of those persons?

In this chapter we examine the ways in which people are similar in personality—and the ways they *think* they're similar in personality—to their friends and spouses.

Similarity Beyond Personality

Before we get to personality characteristics, let's consider some other ways in which you're probably pretty similar to your friends and spouse. We bet that for the most part, your friends and your spouse are similar to you in characteristics such as age, educational level, religious affiliation (or lack thereof), and ethnic background. Any one of those people may differ from you in some of those ways, but on the whole you probably have more in common with them, demographically speaking, than with the average person.

Why is this? One important reason is that when people go to work or school or church or social gatherings, most of the people around them have backgrounds similar to their own. People naturally end up with friends and spouses who share their backgrounds. This happens even if people aren't trying to select social partners who are similar to them.

But most people are even more similar to their spouses and friends—at least in some ways—than to the average person in their broader social surroundings. One example of this is physical attractiveness: on the whole, spouses are more similar in physical attractiveness than two people picked at random would be. This is true even though we can all think of some couples in which one partner is much more attractive than the other.

Some researchers have studied how it is that romantic partners tend to be similar in physical attractiveness. One study followed more than 120 couples over a period of nine months and found that any given couple was more likely to break up when the partners were mismatched for physical attractiveness.[1] Moreover, the more attractive partner of a couple had more opposite-sex friends than did the less attractive partner, which suggests that the more attractive partner had more options for alternative partners and hence a stronger incentive for ending the relationship. Apparently, mate selection is something like a competitive marketplace where people tend to end up with partners whose attractiveness is similar to their own. Of course, attractiveness is not the only characteristic that people desire in a mate, so high levels of other characteristics can compensate for lower attractiveness, and vice versa. Still, physical attractiveness is apparently an important part of a person's overall "mate value" as perceived by others.

Physical attractiveness is a characteristic that pretty much everyone desires in a mate—other things being equal, most people want a mate who is physically attractive. But not all characteristics work this way. For some traits, there is no universally agreed "better" direction, and for most of those traits people prefer a mate who is similar to themselves. Consider religiosity: religious people want religious mates, and people who aren't religious want mates who aren't religious either. You've probably noticed that hard-core atheists rarely marry religious fundamentalists. Such a marriage would make good material for a television sitcom, but it probably wouldn't work. Researchers consistently find that in most marriages, spouses are similar in their level of religiosity.[2] And of course, highly religious people prefer highly religious mates of the *same* religion.[3]

When it comes to the matching of romantic partners, political attitudes are a lot like religious beliefs. People with left-wing attitudes tend to pair off with each other, and so do people with right-wing political attitudes. Couples such as the now-separated Maria Shriver and Arnold Schwarzenegger—she a Democrat, he a Republican—are much less common than couples who have similar political orientations. The similarity between spouses for political ideology is almost as strong as for religiosity.

BOX 6-1   Why Are Spouses Similar in Beliefs and Attitudes?

If spouses are similar in their beliefs and attitudes, does this really mean that like-minded people tend to find one another—in other words, does it mean that spouses were similar even before they met? The matching of similar spouses could happen in some other ways. For example, the viewpoints of one or both spouses may tend to converge over the years. (Even if people were paired off at random, you might still expect partners to become more alike as the months and years go by.) Or perhaps relationships are more likely to break up when the partners' views are just too far apart. (Again, even if people were paired off at random, you might still expect the most durable relationships to be those between people who happen to have similar beliefs and attitudes.)

Some research has tested these possibilities. In one study of over 500 couples, the participants completed surveys of religiosity and political attitudes on occasions 17 years apart.[4] The researchers found that the spouses were just as similar when they were first surveyed as they were many years later. This means that there wasn't any gradual convergence between the spouses as their marriage progressed. Also, the spouses who had divorced or separated—about one-sixth of the sample—were just as similar as the spouses who stayed together. So it wasn't the case that there were lots of ill-fated relationships between partners with opposite viewpoints; instead, such couples had rarely even formed in the first place. This isn't to say that marriages between partners of strongly opposing attitudes would necessarily work. Probably the reason why there are so few couples of this kind is that people usually rule out such relationships as unworkable before they even get started.

Similarity—and Perceived Similarity—in Friends

So much for attitudes. But what about personality? Are spouses similar in personality traits in the sense described in this book? Or do opposites attract? Or is matching completely random? And—in case we become too narrowly focused on romantic relationships—what about friends? Do we generally choose friends whose personalities are similar, on balance, to our own? Or do we pick friends who are opposite to us in some aspects of personality, as if we were seeking friends whose personalities would complement our own?

In the early 2000s, we did a series of research projects that gave us a great deal of interesting data on these questions. As mentioned in the previous chapter, we collected lots of personality data from pairs of closely acquainted people—usually pairs of close friends, sometimes boyfriend/girlfriend couples. As you'll recall, we found fairly high correlations between self-reports and observer reports of the six personality factors. This meant that the students tended to agree with each other in their (independent) assessments of each other's personalities.

Eventually, we realized that these data could also be used to examine the topic of similarity in personality between friends or romantic partners. Remember that in these studies, the participants in each pair completed the personality inventory twice: once to describe their own personality, and once to describe the other person's personality. Suppose that two friends, Jack and Jill, are participants in our study. First Jack and Jill each provide self-reports using our personality inventory; then each provides observer reports of the other person using the same inventory. To find out how much the self-reports on a given trait agree with the observer reports, we simply compare Jack's self-reports with Jill's observer reports about Jack, and vice versa (see Figure 6-1).

But if we want to know how similar our participants are on a given trait, we will instead compare Jack's self-reports and Jill's self-reports (see Figure 6-2). This is the same similarity we were talking about earlier in this chapter—how similar two friends are in a given personality trait.[5]

And finally, if we want to know how similar our participants seem to think they are to each other on a given trait, we compare Jack's self-report with Jack's observer report about Jill, and vice versa. These correlations tell us how similar Jack *thinks* Jill is to him, or how much similarity is implicitly "perceived" or "assumed" by Jack (see Figure 6–3). That is, even though we haven't explicitly asked Jack about how similar he and Jill are, these correlations indicate how much his report about Jill's personality resembles his report about his own personality.

FIGURE 6–1   Self/Observer Agreement

FIGURE 6–2   Similarity

FIGURE 6–3   Perceived Similarity

We searched the personality literature for any previous investigations on similarity and perceived similarity. But we couldn't find many, and the few that existed hadn't found much similarity in personality between friends, or even between spouses, and hadn't found much assumed or perceived similarity either. So we realized that we could learn something new from our data.

When we looked at the correlations between the self-reports of the two friends of each pair, we found that the friends were usually somewhat similar in two of the HEXACO factors: H and O. The degree of similarity was only modest: the correlations were about .25 for both factors.[6] But for the other four factors, there was very little similarity.

What this meant was that the more genuine and unassuming university students (those high in H) tended to find each other as friends—at least at a somewhat higher-than-chance level—and that the more devious and pretentious university students (those low in H) tended to do the same. Likewise, the more inquisitive and complex university students (those high in O) also tended (somewhat) to attract each other as friends, as did the more conventional and unimaginative university students (those low in O). Maybe this doesn't sound so surprising, but what makes these results so interesting is that for the other four personality factors, this tendency was much weaker. For those other dimensions, it was as if the friend pairs were forming almost at random.[7]

The results were even more striking when we examined the amount of perceived similarity between friends, by checking the correlations between people's self-reports and their observer reports about their friends: people perceived their friends as being quite similar to them in the H and O factors, with correlations around .40 (a bit higher for H and a bit lower for O). In other words, the *perceived* similarity between friends for H and O was even greater than the *actual* similarity. But for the other four factors, there was no such perceived similarity.

Putting these two sets of findings together, we can say that friends are somewhat similar in their levels of H and O—but not as similar as they apparently *think* they are. To some extent, friends are correct in perceiving some similarity between themselves in the H and O factors. But they also tend to perceive more similarity than there really is. And for the other four factors, the friends (on average) are neither similar nor opposite, nor do they see each other as similar or opposite.

Personality, Values, and Relationships

These findings still left us with a question: Why these two factors? Why should friends be similar (and perceive themselves to be even more similar) on these two aspects of personality, and only on these two? A couple of years later, we had some ideas and a good opportunity to test them. With our graduate students, Julie Pozzebon and Beth Visser, we began a study of people's "personal values" in relation to the HEXACO personality factors. Personal values is one of the few topics in psychology that can be said to be uniquely human. Researchers can study learning, or perception, or motivation, or intelligence, or even personality in many other non-human animals. For example, there are many scientific reports about "personality" traits for such animals as chimpanzees, dogs, various kinds of fish and birds, and octopuses. Apparently, the personality traits of individuals in those kinds of animals can be measured reliably; furthermore, the differences between individuals are stable across time and are genetically inherited. By contrast, humans seem to be the only animals to have values—ideals about which goals ought to matter in life. By investigating values, we would be able to test our ideas about why some personality traits exhibit similarity and perceived similarity between friends.

What are the main differences among people in their personal values? Researchers have found two broad dimensions: the first factor represents the relative importance one places on individuality and novelty as opposed to conformity and tradition; the second represents the relative importance one places on equality and the welfare of others as opposed to one's own power, wealth, and success.[8] In other words, there are two main ways in which people can differ from one another in their values: one way is that some people prefer independence and change whereas others want to respect authority and preserve tradition; the other is that some people emphasize caring and sharing whereas others are concerned only with their own gain.

You can probably predict how these two dimensions of values were related to the major dimensions of personality: the first was related to the O factor, the second to the H factor. Apparently, people's values are a function of their personalities, but mainly just these two aspects of personality, as the relations with the other four personality factors were weak. So we had finally found an important feature shared by H and O but not by the other four HEXACO factors: the H and O factors, much more than the others, underlie our choices regarding which goals are worth pursuing throughout one's life.

But if the link with values is what explains why friends are similar (and see themselves as similar) in H and O, we should also find similarity (and perceived similarity) for the values dimensions. We checked this out, and sure enough, the pattern of similarity and perceived similarity for the value dimensions was the same as we had found for the H and O factors. People prefer to associate with those who have similar values, and this is probably because these values are so important to one's sense of identity. We define ourselves, in part, in terms of how we think people should relate to one another and to the broader society. Because our personal value system is an important part of who we are, it's an important element in forming our friendships and romantic relationships.[9]

We're not saying that most people consciously decide to start or to continue their relationships by thinking, "Well, this person appears to have values similar to mine, therefore I will choose this person as my friend." Not many people operate in this way. Our point instead is that people simply find that they like each other better when they're on the same wavelength about the things that matter in life, even though they don't necessarily realize that this is influencing their liking for each other.

This explanation also fits neatly with another finding about perceived similarity. People should see their friends or romantic partners as similar to themselves, because those are close, meaningful relationships. In contrast, people shouldn't see so much similarity in other people—say, co-workers or classmates or neighbours—with whom they are fairly well acquainted but not particularly close. And people shouldn't see much similarity either in people whose personalities they can observe but with whom there isn't any relationship at all, such as fictional characters. We tested these ideas out in a couple of studies. In the first, we found that the level of perceived similarity in H and O was much lower for co-workers and classmates and neighbours than for close friends and romantic partners. In the second, we found that there was no perceived similarity at all when we asked our participants to report on the personalities of two familiar television characters (specifically, Ross and Rachel from *Friends*, a popular US sitcom of the 2000s).

All of these results have an interesting practical implication. According to an old Korean saying, we should "look at the friends to learn about the person." Our results suggest that this proverb is true—if we mean the H and O factors of personality, and the values associated with those factors. We could probably get a fairly good idea of a person's levels of H and O by averaging that person's closest friends' levels of each factor.[10] And we could get an even more accurate idea by averaging the levels of H and O that the person *attributes* to his or her friends.

The links between personality and values help us understand why friends tend to be similar—and to perceive each other as similar—in the H and O factors of personality. Those results also open the door to a couple of other domains in which the H and O factors are implicated: politics and religion. These are the topics of the next two chapters.

7

POLITICS

People often say that if you want to get along well with others, you should avoid discussing religion and politics. They say that when you're meeting your new boss, or your new neighbours, or your future in-laws, it's better not to start declaring all your opinions about religious and political matters. You're bound to differ with them on some questions, and those disagreements could lead to a lot of ill feeling.

That is probably good advice. Many people take political and religious questions very seriously. Even when people don't have any personal stake in an issue, they can still have passionate opinions about it. By contrast, people are much less impassioned about factual matters that don't have any obvious political or religious implications. For example, it took more than 30 years for Richard Dawkins's seminal science book, *The Selfish Gene,* to sell a million copies, whereas it took only two years for the same author's anti-religious book, *The God Delusion,* to reach the million mark. Likewise, the American linguistic scholar Noam Chomsky is far more famous for his criticisms of US foreign policy than for his groundbreaking scientific work on language acquisition.

Why do so many of us care so much about political and religious matters? The most likely answer is that political and religious attitudes reflect our basic values—our ideas about how to live and how to relate to other people and to the world. Because these values are so central to our sense of who we are, it's satisfying when people agree with our attitudes, and it's disconcerting when they don't.[1] When people choose partners of any kind, they gravitate toward those who share their political and religious attitudes. For example, as we mentioned at the beginning of the previous chapter, spouses tend to be very similar, on average, in their political and religious views.

In the previous chapter, we explained how the major factors of personality—particularly H and O—underlie the two main trade-offs in people's value systems. In this chapter, we discuss the role of personality in shaping our political attitudes.

Right-Wing Authoritarianism (RWA) and Social Dominance Orientation (SDO)

Researchers who study political attitudes have found that people's attitudes can be predicted very well by just two variables. Those variables are called Right-Wing Authoritarianism (RWA) and Social Dominance Orientation (SDO). Both are assessed by self-report scales. To give you an idea of what these scales measure, we've listed some of the items on each scale in Table 7-1.

First let's consider RWA, which was developed by Bob Altemeyer.[2] People who have high levels of RWA show three related

TABLE 7–1 Example Items from the Right-Wing Authoritarianism
and Social Dominance Orientation Scales

Right-Wing Authoritarianism (RWA)

Everyone should have their own lifestyle, religious beliefs, and sexual
preferences, even if it makes them different from everyone else. (R)

The only way our country can get through the crisis ahead is to get back
to our traditional values, put some tough leaders in power, and silence the
troublemakers spreading bad ideas.

The facts on crime, sexual immorality, and the recent public disorders all show
that we have to crack down harder on deviant groups and troublemakers if we
are going to save our moral standards and preserve law and order.

The established authorities generally turn out to be right about things, while the
radicals and protestors are usually just "loudmouths" showing off their ignorance.

Our country needs free thinkers who have the courage to defy traditional ways,
even if this upsets many people. (R)

Social Dominance Orientation (SDO)

Some groups of people are simply inferior to others.

To get ahead in life, it is sometimes necessary to step on other groups.

Sometimes other groups must be kept in their place.

We should do what we can to equalize conditions for different groups. (R)

All groups should be given an equal chance in life. (R)

Note: "R" indicates a reverse-keyed statement, meaning that disagreement contributes to higher
scores on the scale. RWA items from Altemeyer (1981, 1996); SDO items from Pratto et al. (1994).

tendencies: they conform to conventional norms, they obey the
established authorities, and they support aggression by those
authorities against people who don't conform or who don't obey.
In short, high RWA people tend to disapprove of people and ideas
that challenge the accepted beliefs and structure of society. In the
16th century they would have disliked the heliocentric theory of
Copernicus. In the 19th century they would have disliked Darwin's

Theory of Evolution (come to think of it, many of them still do). High-RWA people in North America today have a predictable pattern of views on political issues: many of them oppose the legalization of (among other things) abortion and doctor-assisted suicide as well as same-sex marriage and recreational drugs.

Next let's consider SDO, which was developed by Felicia Pratto and Jim Sidanius.[3] People who are high in SDO generally want some groups of people (presumably their own) to have higher status and greater wealth and power than other groups. In other words, they prefer hierarchy to equality, both within and between societies. In the 19th century they would have opposed the abolition of serfdom or slavery (unless, of course, they themselves were serfs or slaves). In the early 20th century they would have opposed workplace safety laws. High-SDO people in North America today generally oppose state-run social welfare systems as well as public funding for health care and for higher education, and they generally oppose assistance for foreign countries and for other ethnic groups.

RWA and SDO aren't strongly related to each other, but both are strongly related to political orientation. When people are asked to place themselves on a scale from "left wing" to "right wing," or from "liberal" to "conservative," left-wing or liberal people are likely to score low in both RWA and SDO, and the right-wing or conservative people are likely to score high in both.[4] It's not surprising that the RWA scale predicts how right-wing someone is, but the SDO scale predicts this almost as strongly. For example, one large-scale study of US citizens found that people's self-placement on a scale from "liberal" to "conservative" correlated over .50 with RWA and about .40 with SDO. Again, what makes this finding especially interesting is that RWA and SDO are not so strongly related to each other—in this particular study, the correlation was a little more than .30.[5]

We realize that the above results place politically conservative persons in a somewhat unfavourable light. But we should note that some people who hold conservative views are not particularly high in RWA or in SDO. Moreover, some of the correlates of political conservatism are more desirable: conservatives tend to be slightly happier than liberals and to be slightly more satisfied with life; they also tend to have a somewhat greater sense of personal control and personal responsibility.[6]

Besides being related to people's general political orientations, RWA and SDO predict a variety of more specific attitudes.[7] For example, both are associated with blind patriotism ("My country right or wrong!") and with support for the war. (Which war? The current one.) Note, however, that RWA and SDO are associated with different *reasons* for supporting wars: high-RWA persons see the world as a dangerous place in which enemies threaten the values and safety of one's people, whereas high-SDO persons see the world as a competitive place in which enemies must be defeated for the sake of the status, power, and wealth of one's people.

In addition, RWA and SDO are both associated with dislike of minority ethnic groups, of gays and lesbians, and of women's rights. The combination of RWA and SDO can predict those attitudes very well—considerably better than either variable on its own.[8] Altemeyer has put it this way: if there were a Prejudice Olympics, the gold medal would go to people who are high in both RWA and SDO (the "double highs," as he calls them), and people high in SDO only or high in RWA only would win the silver and bronze, respectively. People low in both would finish out of the medals, but we think they'd be happy just to have met so many wonderful people from all over the world.

O and Right-Wing Authoritarianism

How do RWA and SDO relate to the major dimensions of personality? First, as you'd probably expect, RWA is related to low levels of the O factor. This means that people who are more socially conservative—who favour the conventional social structure and conventional norms—tend to be lower in O. As we explained in Chapter 3, high-O people don't mind things that are new and unusual, so they're more likely to try eating strange foods or visiting faraway countries or using new technologies. And high-O people especially like new and unusual ideas—perhaps too much, in some cases—so they aren't strongly tied to conventional notions of how society should be structured.

The link between the O factor and low RWA is moderately strong, but it's far from perfect. You can probably think of some low-O people who don't have socially conservative views and some high-O people who do. (You could probably find some of the latter in the Vatican and some of the former in Las Vegas.) And even though people with higher levels of O have a *predisposition* to favour social change, there are many other variables that can influence one's political perspective. For example, a high-O person who visits some extremely chaotic country might conclude that traditional values are needed to maintain a functioning society even though his or her personal taste is for greater individual freedom. Nevertheless, the point is that lower levels of O usually go along with higher levels of social conservatism.

One interesting twist on this trend is that the link between O and political attitudes gets stronger as people get older. Among people in their late teens and twenties, lower O is only weakly related to social conservatism. Among middle-aged people, this link is much stronger. It's as if one's level of O exerts a stronger influence on one's political thinking as one gets older: low-O people gravitate toward socially conservative positions, and high-O people drift away from those positions.

In one of our research projects,[9] we studied personality and political attitudes in three countries: Canada, South Korea, and the United States. Our hypothesis was that in all three countries, RWA should be more strongly related to O than to any of the other personality factors. The results supported this hypothesis, but the links between RWA and O weren't the same across the three countries. In our Korean and Canadian samples, the correlation between O and RWA was modest (about –.20); in the US sample, the correlation was much stronger (about –.50). This was a pretty big difference, and it's all the more striking given that it can't be explained by cultural differences—the USA is culturally much more similar to Canada than to Korea.

But there was an important difference between our US participants and our participants from Canada and Korea: the US participants were much older. All of them were middle-aged adults, most of them university graduates, and their average age was over 50. By contrast, our Canadian and Korean participants were university students whose average age was around 20. So, the difference between the US results and the Korean and Canadian results suggests that as people get older, their levels of O have stronger effects on their social conservatism.

Why would the link between low O and RWA become stronger after young adulthood? We can get some hints from research in behaviour genetics, which examines how the differences between people can be explained by their different genes and their different environments (see Box 3–3). According to this research, differences among adolescents or young adults in political and religious views are due in large part to differences among the households in which they were raised.[10] In other words, parents' attitudes have a big influence on the level of social conservatism of their adolescent and young adult children.

After young adulthood, however, the influence of parents' attitudes becomes weaker and genetic influences become stronger. Apparently, what happens is that from young adulthood on, people's religious and political views become less strongly influenced by those of the parents who raised them. Instead, adults gradually develop attitudes that are more consistent with their personality characteristics—characteristics that have a genetic basis. In the case of socially conservative views, this largely means that the O factor exerts a stronger effect after young adulthood. Consider an 18-year-old who shares the socially conservative views of his or her parents. If that 18-year-old is high in O, he or she is likely to become lower in RWA during later adulthood; if low in O, he or she will probably maintain the parents' conservative views.

The link between RWA and low O explains some interesting facts that you've probably already noticed in everyday life. One such fact is that academics and artists tend to be left-wing in their political orientation. Consider academics—specifically, university professors. One large survey found that 44% of US university professors described themselves as liberal and only 9% as conservative (the other 47% were "moderate"). In contrast, a large survey of the general US public found that only 22% were liberals, whereas 35% were conservatives (with the other 43% moderates).[11]

How does the O factor explain the left-wing political views of professors? People high in O tend to be intellectually curious, and such curiosity is perhaps the defining trait of the typical professor. At the same time, as we saw above, high O underlies socially liberal attitudes, including rejection of traditional religiosity. Thus, it's not surprising that professors would be politically liberal.

One way to view the role of O is by examining differences between academic disciplines regarding how left-wing their professors are. First of all, the most left-wing disciplines are generally those within the humanities and social sciences, such as sociology, English literature, and philosophy.[12] People who are interested in these areas of knowledge tend to be very high in O.[13] Also, within any given area of knowledge, the more left-wing professors are usually found in the more theoretical or pure disciplines, and the more right-wing professors in the more practical or applied disciplines. For example, professors in economics are more liberal than those in banking and finance, professors in physics are more liberal than those in engineering, and professors in biology are more liberal than those in medicine. In these cases, it's likely that high levels of O have attracted some persons to the theoretical disciplines and that those same high levels of O also favour a left-wing political orientation.

Like professors, artists tend to be very left-wing in their political orientation. (And among professors, those who teach in the fine or performing arts are among the most left-wing, rivalling even the sociologists.)[14] As with professors, the left-wing tendencies of artists can be understood in terms of the O factor. Artists tend to be very high in the traits that define O—such as aesthetic appreciation, creativity, curiosity, and unconventionality—and these same traits are together related to socially liberal attitudes and to the rejection of traditional religiosity. Of course, some low-O people have some talent for painting or sculpting or for playing a musical instrument. But being an artist—creating a work of art for the sake of evoking emotions and ideas—is inherently a high-O endeavour. For this reason, highly original works of art rarely emphasize conservative values. And most famous artists—from Pablo Picasso to Charlie Chaplin—have been left-wing in their political views.

The O factor also explains some other characteristics of left-wing and right-wing people. For example, one group of researchers wondered whether people's political views could be inferred from the kinds of possessions they kept in their living spaces.[15] The researchers went to a university dormitory and, with the students' permission, carefully inspected the students' rooms, counting various kinds of objects. When the researchers examined the rooms, they didn't yet know the political views of the students. But they asked those students in a separate survey to place themselves on a scale running from liberal to conservative. (This study was done in the United States, so "liberal" and "conservative" mean left-wing and right-wing.)

The researchers found that the more liberal students' rooms had more books and music CDs—as well as a wider *variety* of books and music CDs—than did the more conservative students' rooms. The liberal students also had more movie tickets and travel tickets. Notice that the everyday possessions in liberal students' rooms suggest wide intellectual and artistic interests—expressions of high O. By contrast, the more conservative students' rooms had more flags (especially US flags) and more sports-related decor than did the more liberal students' rooms, which suggested a

---

BOX 7–1   Political Orientation, Sexual Orientation, and the O Factor

Political orientation is related to sexual orientation. For example, in the 2008 US elections, 80% of gay, lesbian, or bisexual voters supported Democratic Party candidates for the House of Representatives; only 19% supported Republican Party candidates. The corresponding numbers for heterosexual voters were 53% and 44%.[16] One likely reason for this pattern is that the Democrats are viewed as much more supportive of gay and lesbian rights than are the Republicans. But even in the absence of these important policy differences, it's likely that most gay and lesbian voters would still favour left-wing over right-wing parties. On average, gay men and lesbians have higher levels of the O factor than do heterosexual men and women.[17] The difference isn't huge, and even among persons very high in O, the large majority are heterosexual. Still, gay men and lesbians are overrepresented among high-O persons, especially among people in the arts.[18] Because higher levels of the O factor are strongly associated with preferences for the political left, most gay and lesbian voters would favour left-wing parties even when matters of sexual orientation are not among the election issues.

more conventional orientation. The conservative students also had more event calendars, postage stamps, string and thread, and ironing boards and irons—possessions suggesting orderliness and planning ahead. This latter result is consistent with other findings of a modest link between the C factor and political orientation, which we'll discuss later on.

H and Social Dominance Orientation

Now let's turn from RWA to SDO, the other major political attitude variable. As you'll recall, high-SDO people favour a hierarchical society in which some groups dominate other groups. The links between SDO and personality are also close to what you'd expect: SDO relates mainly to the low levels of the H factor, meaning that high-H people generally oppose social hierarchies.[19] The tendency for high-H people to be low in SDO makes sense in light of the traits that define the H factor, as discussed in Chapters 3 and 4. High-H people are straightforward and fair in their dealings with others, and they don't want superior status and wealth and power. Therefore, they dislike the idea of stepping on other groups or of keeping other groups in their place.

By the way, even though the H factor is a pretty good predictor of egalitarian views, the link isn't perfect, or even close to perfect. Some people who are low in H might adopt egalitarian attitudes if it's in their interest to do so—in fact, being the high-profile leader of a left-wing political party might be an attractive prospect for a low-H person who holds no genuine commitment to the principle of social equality. And some people who are high in H (and low in SDO) might decide—rightly or wrongly—that too much economic equality or too much multiculturalism causes problems.

High-SDO people share with low-H people a willingness to make decisions that by most standards would be grossly unethical. For example, one study showed that high-SDO students, just like low-H people, reported that they'd be willing to make money by exporting dangerous products to a developing country[20]—a finding similar to that observed for low-H people (as we'll discuss in Chapter 9). The same study also examined what happened when decisions were made by pairs of people in which one member of each pair was arbitrarily designated as the leader. The results showed that the pairs most likely to make unethical decisions were those that combined a high SDO leader with a high RWA follower—a combination that Altemeyer has called the "lethal union." A country whose high-SDO leaders are supported by high-RWA citizens would be a prime candidate for starting aggressive wars—wars that the leaders would cynically justify as necessary for the security of the nation, simply as a way to rally the population.

We examined the link between H and SDO in the study we mentioned earlier, based on samples from Canada, Korea, and United States. In all three samples, low H was associated with high SDO. Now, you might recall that the link between low O and high RWA was stronger in the sample of middle-aged US adults than in the samples of Canadian and Korean university students. But in contrast, the correlation between low H and high SDO was similar across all three samples, averaging nearly −.40. It seems that people's personalities—specifically, their levels of the H factor—influence their attitudes toward social inequality to about the same extent regardless of their age. Again, this wasn't the case for personality in relation to social conservatism: low levels of O were related to social conservatism only modestly in young adults, but more strongly in middle-aged adults.

Why the difference? Apparently, the influence of parents' attitudes on young people's attitudes is weaker for issues of social inequality than for issues of social change. Researchers typically find that similarity between parents and their (young adult) children is much stronger for RWA than for SDO.[21] If you're a parent, you may have some important influence on your children's attitudes toward traditional or modern values, but you probably have much less influence on your children's attitudes about hierarchy or equality in society.

BOX 7–2   Personality and Politics: It Depends on the Context

All of the findings we've described this chapter have been based on people who belong to mainstream or majority groups in modern societies. But these findings don't necessarily apply when we consider other groups or other kinds of societies.

First, consider low-H people who happen to belong to a disadvantaged minority group. Those people might claim to be ardent egalitarians, denouncing the inequalities of their society. But this egalitarianism would simply be a cynical reflection of their own personal interest in improving their low social status. Such people would still favour hierarchies within their own group, as long as those hierarchies put them at the top. (Low-H people from low-status groups might sometimes favour social hierarchies for the society as a whole, in cases when it's possible for them—individually or as a group—to move into positions of higher status.) Likewise, consider low-O people who happen to belong to a minority group that is alienated from mainstream society. Those people might well become rebels and dissidents, trying to undermine the authorities and conventions of the mainstream group. But they wouldn't approve of such dissent within their *own* group; instead, they would expect the members of their group to obey its rules and leaders.

Now consider a different kind of society—specifically, a communist society of the kind that dominated much of the world during the second half of the 20th century. The official ideology of communist countries emphasizes economic and racial equality, so the low-H people of those societies probably wouldn't openly favour a hierarchy based on social class or on ethnicity. But those people would still pursue status and wealth within the communist system, and they would likely favour an aggressive foreign policy aimed at dominating other countries. Also, because communist societies discourage organized religion, the low-O citizens of those countries wouldn't be exposed to traditional religious teachings. But those people would still support the conventional norms of morality within their society, and their obedience would be directed toward the Communist Party and its dogma.[22]

Personality and Political Party Support

We mentioned above that you can predict people's attitudes on many social and political issues by knowing their levels of RWA and SDO. People who are high in both SDO and RWA are the most right-wing (or conservative), and people who are low in both SDO and RWA are the most left-wing (or liberal). (People who are high in one and low in the other tend to be in the middle overall, even though they have quite different combinations of left-wing and right-wing views.) So, does this mean that the supporters of different political parties are different in personality? Given that SDO is related to low H, and given that RWA is related to low O, you might expect supporters of left-wing parties to be higher in both H and O than supporters of right-wing parties. Is this true?

The answer differs a bit from one country to the next. In a study of Italian voters, Antonio Chirumbolo and Luigi Leone found that those who voted for right-wing parties were, on average, lower in H and lower in O than those who voted for left-wing parties—a result that follows the above logic exactly. Two other studies in Germany found very similar results.[23] As expected, these differences were only modest in size. But some data from US voters—specifically, of middle-class, white, Anglo, mainly Christian residents of Oregon—gave somewhat different findings. The right-wing (Republican) voters did average lower in O than the left-wing (Democratic) voters. Also, the Republican voters averaged somewhat higher in C than did the Democratic voters.[24] However, the Republicans and Democrats averaged about the same in H.

The lack of any link between H and political party preference in the US study is somewhat puzzling. If low H relates to SDO, and if SDO in turn relates to right-wing (Republican) support, then you'd expect Republicans, on average, to be somewhat low in H. So why don't we find this? Why were the Republicans no less and no more honest and humble than the Democrats?

Apparently, some mystery variable is balancing out what would otherwise be a tendency toward low H in Republicans, who tend to be high in SDO.

To understand what's happening, consider the following sports analogy. Suppose that you have a really excellent vertical jump. Other things being equal, a better jumper should be a better volleyball player, so we'd expect you to be an above-average volleyball player. But if in fact you're just an average volleyball player, then something else must be balancing out the effect of your jumping ability. For example, height also contributes to many aspects of volleyball performance, so if you're much shorter than average, then perhaps this could be cancelling out the effect of your excellent vertical jump.

What is it, then, that balances out the effect of SDO so that Republicans aren't any lower in H? We suspect that it's religion. The more religious Americans tend to support the Republican Party, and on average, religious Americans are slightly above average in the H factor. If SDO and religiosity were both associated with being Republican, but if SDO and religiosity had *opposite* links with H, then Republicans would be no higher or lower in H than Democrats would be. And this is essentially what we find.

We've just revealed that high-H people are slightly more likely than low-H people to be religious. If this makes you wonder exactly how personality is related to religious and spiritual beliefs, stay tuned for our next chapter.

8

RELIGION

Some people don't believe in any beings or forces that are beyond the laws of nature. They reject the ideas of a God or gods, of souls or spirits, of miracles or magic powers. But other people are utterly certain of their beliefs in supernatural forces, and these beliefs may pervade almost every aspect of their lives.

The topic of this chapter is religiosity. We'll consider the role of personality in explaining which people will be religious and how they will express their religiosity. We'll also examine how religions encourage the expression of certain personality characteristics.

But we should begin by explaining why religiosity is not itself a personality characteristic. First of all, a person's religiosity depends ultimately on his or her beliefs about the supernatural or spiritual world; by contrast, a person's level of a personality disposition doesn't depend on any particular set of beliefs. Also, religiosity often involves following a way of life that is meant to achieve harmony with some higher power—typically God, or the universe itself. A religious way of life involves a wide range of behaviours that wouldn't otherwise go together—for example, a given religion may prescribe various rules about what to eat or when to work or whom to marry.[1] By contrast, the behaviours associated with a given personality disposition usually share some obvious similarities; for example, the X factor of personality involves behaviours such as leading, entertaining, and socializing with others.

Personality and Religious Beliefs

So, who believes in the supernatural, and who doesn't? In modern countries, personality characteristics give us only vague hints as to which people will be believers. There is a weak tendency for people who are nicer or more soft-hearted to be more likely to believe in some supernatural forces. In a study we conducted with our graduate student Babatunde Ogunfowora, we found that belief in the supernatural was modestly associated with higher levels of the H, A, and E factors.[2] One potential reason for these associations is that nicer, more soft-hearted people like to believe there is something more to life than mere physical existence. For example, they like the idea that people have souls that will survive their bodies, and they like the idea that people who are separated by death will meet in an afterlife. By contrast, people who are lower in H, A, and E—people who are not quite so nice, or a bit less soft-hearted—may lack this motivation to believe in an afterlife and may even take some satisfaction from rejecting those comforting beliefs. Still, the relations between personality and supernatural beliefs are rather weak. (In case you'd like some numbers, the correlations of H and A and E with belief in the supernatural are only in the .20s.) This means that many people don't fit the trend: you can find a lot of very nice, soft-hearted people who reject any belief in the supernatural, and a lot of not-so-nice, hard-hearted people who accept such beliefs quite decidedly.

The link between soft-heartedness and supernatural beliefs comes from our own data, but other researchers have found similar results. In a review of over 60 previous studies, Vassilis Saroglou found that, on average, religious people are slightly more soft-hearted than non-religious people.[3]

Now, given that personality and religiosity are related, you might wonder which one influences the other. Do personality traits influence religiosity, or do religious beliefs influence personality? So far, the evidence is very limited, but it mostly favours the former direction of influence. When researchers have followed people over many years, they've found that personality traits early in life predict religiosity later in life, more than the other way around.[4]

One other hint that personality influences religious beliefs comes from the pattern of sex differences in these variables. On average, women are somewhat more soft-hearted than men and slightly more likely to believe in the supernatural. If we control for the sex difference in soft-heartedness, the sex difference in supernatural beliefs is reduced by about half. But if we instead control for the sex difference in supernatural beliefs, the sex difference in soft-heartedness is diminished only slightly. This pattern of results suggests that women are somewhat more strongly attracted to supernatural beliefs by virtue of being somewhat more soft-hearted than men.[5]

The idea that religious people tend to be soft-hearted is partly consistent—but only partly—with some claims from a 2006 book by the social scientist Arthur Brooks.[6] He noted the results of a survey that indicated that religious Americans (i.e., those who go to their house of worship nearly every week) donated three-and-a-half times more money to charities than did non-religious Americans ($2,210 versus $642). He also stated that the greater generosity of religious Americans persists even when one considers only those donations that were made to non-religious charities. Technically, this statement is true, but the gap between religious and non-religious Americans in secular giving, as reported by Brooks, is quite small: religious Americans donated only about 10% more than did non-religious Americans to secular charities ($532 to $467). So, religious Americans give more—but only slightly more—money to secular charities than do non-religious Americans. This small difference is about what you'd expect given the modest link between religiosity and soft-heartedness.[7]

Relatively few people reject *all* supernatural beliefs. Even in countries where most people don't belong to an organized religion, most people still believe in some supernatural beings or forces. But if personality is only modestly related to belief in the supernatural, what is it that determines which people will be hard-core skeptics, rejecting all supernatural beliefs? One candidate is exposure to science. The very mission of science is to explain our surroundings—including the origins of humans, of life, of the Earth, and of the universe—in terms of laws that solely involve natural causes. So as you might expect, scientists are much more likely than other people to reject supernatural beliefs. In one study, 41% of US scientists indicated that they did not believe in God or any other higher power, as opposed to only 4% of the US general public.[8] A similar study found that the proportion of disbelievers was 45% for scientists in general and a remarkably high 72% for members of the National Academy of Sciences, whose members are highly accomplished scientists.[9] Of course, this still leaves many scientists—even many distinguished scientists—who do believe in the supernatural, including some who are devoutly religious. But the proportion of scientists who are skeptics is clearly very high.

The above findings leave open the question of whether it's really the study of science that makes scientists reject belief in the supernatural. It might be instead that scientists are simply the kind of people who would have rejected supernatural beliefs even without any study of science. But the personality characteristics of scientists can't explain their lack of religiosity. As we noted above, personality characteristics are at most only a small part of the story, and in any case scientists aren't so much different in personality from people in general. (The data from Goldberg's sample of Oregon community residents indicate that people with greater interest in scientific careers tend to be somewhat high in the O factor, and slightly low in the "soft-heartedness" factors of H, A, and E. But the differences are small.)

But if the skepticism shown by scientists isn't due to their personalities, you might wonder whether it's their intelligence that's responsible: after all, scientists tend to be smart people. But there's only a modest link between having a high IQ and rejecting the supernatural. One recent large-scale study of US teenagers found that the average IQ among atheists was about 5 points higher than that of the population in general. This means that although atheists are somewhat smarter on average than non-atheists, the difference is not large; for example, more than one-third of non-atheists would have a higher IQ than the average atheist. (In the same study, by the way, agnostics averaged about 3 IQ points higher than the general population. Jews and Anglicans or Episcopalians had average IQs 1 or 2 points higher than those of the atheists, and the average IQ among Catholics was about equal to that of the general population. The more "liberal" Protestant denominations were slightly above average, and the more "dogmatic" Protestant denominations somewhat below average.)[10]

Taken together, all of the above findings suggest that scientists' individual characteristics—their levels of IQ and the major personality factors—aren't the main reasons for their lack of supernatural beliefs. Instead, their skepticism about the supernatural is probably due mostly to their intensive study of science and their commitment to the scientific method.

Traditional Religion versus Mystical Spirituality: The Role of O

Now let's move on to our second question about religion and personality. Among people who do believe in the supernatural, how does personality relate to the style or form of their beliefs—to the way they express their religiosity or spirituality? Here it's the O factor that plays the most important role.

The O factor doesn't tell us much about whether or not a person will believe in the supernatural. People who deny the existence of any and all supernatural forces or beings—people who don't believe in God or souls or spirits or magic or anything outside the natural world—are about equally likely to be high or low in O. What the O factor can tell us, however, is *what kind* of supernatural beliefs people are likely to hold.

On the one hand, low-O people who believe in the supernatural tend to have traditional religious beliefs. Low-O persons prefer strict adherence to the beliefs and practices of the mainstream religious community. For example, in societies having a Christian religious tradition, low-O persons (or at least those low-O persons raised in religious households) are inclined to accept the literal truth of the Bible—to believe in the creation story as given in Genesis, in the existence of God and Satan and heaven and hell, and in the virgin birth and resurrection of Jesus Christ. As you might expect, these low-O believers are very socially conservative.

On the other hand, high-O people who believe in the supernatural tend to have what we call mystically spiritual beliefs. For example, in Western societies, high-O persons are inclined to adopt a variety of magical, occult, or paranormal beliefs, including beliefs in astrology, witchcraft, ghosts, extrasensory perception, and psychokinesis. They're also inclined to adopt teachings from Eastern religions such as Buddhism or Hinduism or from the spiritual traditions of Native American peoples. In general, high-O persons are attracted to new religious movements that emphasize spiritual searching by the individual. These high-O believers, unlike the traditionally religious low-O believers, are inclined to be slightly liberal on social issues.

The O factor thus has moderately strong—and opposite—links with these two forms of supernatural beliefs. In one large-scale study, Gerard Saucier and Katarzyna Skrzypińska found that O correlated about −.25 with traditional religiosity and about .40 with mystical spirituality.[11] So even though O can't tell us whether a person will accept or reject the existence of supernatural beings or forces, it can give us some clues as to which kinds of super-natural beliefs he or she would be more inclined to hold.[12]

The links between O and religious or spiritual beliefs give an interesting insight about the history of religious movements. People who start a new religion or who become its enthusiastic early converts are likely to be high in O. People who maintain an established religion or who become its most devout defenders are likely to be low in O.

Reasons for Religious Observance: The Role of H

We've explained how it's the O factor of personality that plays the biggest role in explaining the style or form of people's beliefs in the supernatural—whether people will be religious traditionalists or spiritual mystics. But the H factor also plays a part in the domain of religion. As we mentioned in the previous chapter, high-H people are slightly more likely than low-H people to be religious. And as we mentioned earlier in this chapter, a likely reason for this link (and for the similar links of the A and E factors with religiosity) is that soft-hearted, sympathetic people tend to favour the ideas that people have souls that will survive their bodies and that people who are separated by death will meet in an afterlife.

But besides having a modest link with religious and spiritual beliefs, the H factor is involved in the reasons people have for *expressing* those beliefs. Consider two people who both belong to the same church or other religious group. Both of them attend religious services regularly, both of them donate money to their religious group and its causes, and both of them observe the rituals of their religion. But the two have utterly different reasons for their outward adherence to the rules of their religious community. For one of those people, these visible signs of religious commitment are genuine expressions of his or her deepest beliefs. For the other person, the same behaviours are merely for public consumption, intended simply to project an image of respectability and to make contacts with people of high status in that community. This person might believe in the tenets of his or her religion, but this belief isn't what motivates his or her public religiosity.

Now, most people who belong to a religious community won't be such clear-cut cases as our two examples above; instead, most will have some mixture of these two reasons for their public displays of religiosity. But some people are clearly more sincere than others in their religious observances. And as you would guess, it's high-H people whose expressions of religious devotion are more genuine, and low-H people whose expressions are more cynical. That said, you can think of some circumstances in which it wouldn't work this way. Imagine a highly religious and highly conformist society that essentially ostracizes people who don't go through the motions of religious observance. In such a society, even high-H non-believers might reluctantly decide that they have no choice but to pretend to be religious.

The link between the H factor and the motivation for religious observance applies to religious leaders as well as to followers. Most people who enter the clergy are genuinely religious, and people who indicate a strong interest in religious vocations are, on average, rather high in H.[13] Nevertheless, there are reasons why at least some low-H people are attracted to the career of religious leader. A religious vocation could provide a path for achieving some position of high status. For example, within a large denomination, one could hope to navigate one's way into the top positions of the hierarchy of religious authorities. And even within small, local religious communities, there is the prospect of wielding considerable influence over one's congregation. In the cases of very low-H people, there is also the potential for financial or sexual exploitation of one's followers. Such cases are well known among established religions but are perhaps especially prevalent among new religious cults. And of course, low-H people with sufficient charisma and organizational skills can aspire to become the next great televangelist, soliciting donations from a vast population of unquestioning followers.

Do Religions Promote High H?

The H factor influences the expression of religiosity; conversely, religious teachings can be designed to influence the expression of the H factor. Most religions encourage the ideal of behaving as a high-H person—being honest and humble in dealings with others. Virtually every major religious tradition has its counterpart of the Golden Rule, often paraphrased from the King James Bible as "Do unto others as you would have them do unto you." But the crucial difference among religions is in how widely this ideal is to be applied: Is everyone to be treated fairly, or only the other members of one's own group?

Some religious teachings encourage believers to act as high-H persons toward co-religionists but as low-H persons toward outsiders. Consider the Old Testament: in the Book of Deuteronomy, the Ten Commandments instruct believers not to commit murder or theft or adultery or perjury. Later chapters of Deuteronomy, however, instruct believers to commit genocide against various other religious groups. For example, "when the Lord your God brings you into the land you are entering to possess and drives out before you many nations … then you must destroy them totally. Make no treaty with them and show them no mercy" (Deuteronomy 7:1–2, NIV). Likewise, "do not leave alive anything that breathes. Completely destroy them … as the Lord your God has commanded you" (Deuteronomy 20:16, NIV).[14] (We should mention, by the way, that religions have no monopoly on genocide: most of the state-sponsored mass murders of the 20th century were inspired by non-religious ideologies.)

In some religious traditions, by contrast, the imperative to treat others fairly is truly universal, with no distinction drawn between co-religionists and outsiders. Consider the Religious Society of Friends, better known as the Quakers. This sect separated from the Church of England during the 17th century and subsequently spread to other areas of the world. Among the defining features of the Quaker movement are its testimonies, which provide principles for how to live. For example, the Testimony of Simplicity urges believers to avoid ostentation and materialism, and hence encourages high-H behaviours. Note that these Quaker testimonies are meant to govern one's interactions with Quakers and non-Quakers alike. The Testimony of Integrity emphasizes telling the truth (and avoiding even indirect deceptions) as well as fair dealing: early Quakers gained reputations as honest businessmen through their practices of paying decent wages to their (non-Quaker) workers and setting fixed prices when selling goods to their (also non-Quaker) customers. The Testimony of Peace encourages pacifism and hence forbids aggression against outgroups. Among the early settlers of North America, the Quakers were known for their peaceful relations—and their scrupulous adherence to treaties—with Native Americans. The Testimony of Equality holds that all persons have equal rights and hence forbids exploitation of outgroups. As early as the 18th century, the Quakers declared their opposition to the slave trade and to slavery itself, and contemporary Quakers continue to advocate for human rights.

Why do some religions encourage high-H behaviours only within the group, whereas others encourage high-H behaviours toward everyone? It may depend in part on whether the religion is suited for high-O people or low-O people. The more dogmatic or fundamentalist movements—low in O—require obedience and conformity; they draw strong distinctions between "us" and "them," with especially strong moral obligations toward the former but few if any toward the latter. By contrast, the more liberal or progressive movements—high in O—aren't much concerned with obedience and conformity; they draw weaker distinctions between us and them, with moral obligations extended toward all.

As we've seen in this chapter, the H factor is implicated in several aspects of people's religious beliefs. In the next chapter, we'll consider three domains in which H is even more strongly involved: money, power, and sex.

9

MONEY, POWER, AND SEX

The behaviour of low-H people is expressed in many aspects of life. Here we'll consider three domains in which people who are very low in H really distinguish themselves: money, power, and sex.

Money

Most people who are low in H will usually try to get money through perfectly legal means, by working and investing. This simply reflects the reality that crime usually doesn't pay. Most low-H people realize that it's hard to get away with theft or fraud for a long time, and they decide that it's better to look for more reliable ways of getting rich. But in principle, they quite like the idea of getting something for nothing, and it doesn't bother them if that particular something comes at someone else's expense. So the people who are most ready to steal and to swindle when the opportunity arises—and the people who do in fact commit most of the acquisitive crimes—are people low in H.

In some of our own research studies, we've asked students to report—confidentially and anonymously—the dollar value of the money and merchandise they've stolen. What we always find is that the people who have stolen the most—whether by shoplifting, by break and enter, by pilfering on the job, or otherwise—are much below average in H. Generally, most of the total amount stolen is accounted for by less than 10% of the students, and on average those students are lower in H than about 80% to 90% of students overall.[1]

Now, you might think it's not really so impressive that the people who say they're low in H are the same people who say they've stolen a lot. Couldn't it all just be a matter of who is willing to admit, or even exaggerate, their own dishonesty? But actually, it isn't. Even when we measure the students' personalities using observer reports—provided by the student's roommate, or best friend, or boyfriend/girlfriend—low levels of H are still related to self-reports of theft. And those self-reports of theft are related to all the various aspects of low H, including the aspects that don't have any obvious, transparent link with theft: the college students who've stolen the most are mainly the same ones who think they're better than others and who like to manipulate people. (For some research that isn't based on participants' admissions of past wrongdoings, see Box 9–1 for a study that relied on direct observations of dishonest behaviour.)

Low H has a fairly strong link with theft (and with crime and delinquency more generally), but that link is far from perfect, for several reasons. On the one hand, some people who are low in H have few opportunities to steal, and some feel rich enough that they have little motivation to do so. And many low-H people have

BOX 9–1   Cheating in the Psychology Lab

In a recent study, Hal Hershfield, Taya Cohen, and Leigh Thompson examined whether people's levels of the H factor—as measured by self-reports on the HEXACO-PI-R—predicted which of them would cheat in a laboratory task. The researchers asked their student research participants to solve a series of eight anagram problems (e.g., unscrambling EFLWOR to form FLOWER). Each participant was promised 50 cents for each anagram that he or she solved. The rules, however, stated that the anagrams must be solved in sequence—in other words, the participant had to solve the first anagram before moving on to the second, then solve the second before going to the third, and so on. The trick was that the second and seventh anagrams were virtually unsolvable, because these were extremely rare words (i.e., MENALD, CAPRIC) that are unknown to almost all students.

After 15 minutes, each participant was asked to count the anagram problems that he or she had solved and to take the corresponding amount of cash from an envelope, in an honour system of payment. Participants who wanted to cheat could feel free to do so, because participation was anonymous and there was no verification of the number of solved problems. But because the second and seventh anagrams were essentially unsolvable, participants who took payment for solving two to six problems must have cheated once, and participants who took payment for solving seven or eight problems must have cheated twice.

The researchers found that low-H participants were more likely to have cheated in taking payment for solving the anagrams. The correlation between the H factor and cheating—about −.35—is actually surprisingly large, given that many other variables could influence cheating behaviour in this particular situation (an extremely low-stakes situation, we might add) and on this particular occasion.[2]

other personality traits that make them cautious about stealing. As we mentioned in Chapter 4, low-H persons who are also low in C and low in E are strong candidates for criminal activity, whereas low-H persons who are high in C and high in E express their dishonesty a lot more prudently.

At the same time, some high-H people occasionally commit dishonest acts. Sometimes a situation is tempting enough that only people very high in H resist the urge to act selfishly. And in some situations, dishonest actions are motivated less by low H than by other characteristics. A young person who wouldn't think of stealing (or cheating, etc.) on his or her own might succumb to peer pressure. Or a young person who has no intrinsic motivation to commit such a crime might do so purely as an act of rebellion against parents or authority figures. Because of these varying circumstances, we can't always be sure that a particular dishonest act was driven by a low level of H in the person who committed that act. To take just one example, many high-H people would steal out of desperation if they or their kin were hungry or cold or sick. This situation confronts very few, if any, of the students in our samples, but it's worth remembering that although a given behaviour can be strongly influenced by a personality trait in one situation, the same behaviour may be almost irrelevant to that personality trait in another situation.

Some ways of studying personality and behaviour allow us to control for situational influences and thereby see the full strength of the link between low H and various dishonest actions. Probably the best such approach is to ask people to respond to hypothetical scenarios that depict some opportunity to act dishonestly for personal gain. By describing the features of these scenarios in just the right way, we can find out how people would act in a prototypical default situation—in the absence of any risk of getting caught, of any truly desperate straits, or of any pressures to conform or to rebel. This approach also allows us to find out how personality would relate to dishonest behaviours of a kind that few people have the opportunity to commit.

One such kind of dishonesty is corporate crime, whereby officials commit crimes that profit their company. This form of dishonest behaviour is interesting for the ways in which it differs from more common crimes. Unlike common theft or robbery, corporate crime is usually committed by people who have high levels of income, education, and occupational status. And unlike common theft or robbery, it often involves massive amounts of money taken from many people.

Few people ever find themselves in a position to commit large-scale corporate crimes. But how many people would do so, given the chance? And how much is personality—particularly a low-H personality—implicated in the willingness to commit those crimes? We've studied this by asking several hundred university students to respond to a series of scenarios in which they take the role of a corporate executive. Each scenario describes an opportunity to maximize the company's profit—and the respondent's income—in a highly unethical way that involves corrupt business practices, risks to public health and safety, or damage to the environment. Here's just one example:

> Suppose that you are in charge of sales for a large corporation that exports telecommunications equipment to countries around the world. Recently, you have been trying to obtain the contract for supplying a new telecom system to Impoveria, a developing nation that has only recently begun to modernize.

In negotiations with the president of Impoveria and his cabinet, you have learned that your company's bid is not the lowest; instead, two of your competitor companies have lower bids. However, the president and his cabinet members have told you that you can still have the contract, if you agree to send back 5% of the money received from the Impoverian government to their own personal bank accounts in Switzerland. It is clear to you that, even with this 5% kickback, your company will still make a substantial profit on this contract, and that you will be seen as the person who made it happen.

Would you recommend that your company agree to the conditions and sign the contract?

(1) Definitely Not   (2) Probably Not
(3) Probably Yes   (4) Definitely Yes

So, how many of our students would put profit ahead of morality? About 15% responded "probably yes" or "definitely yes" to most of the scenarios. Conversely, about 15% responded "definitely not" to most scenarios. (The other 70% mainly responded "probably not"; this means that they leaned toward the ethical option, but not as strongly as you might want our future corporate leaders to do.)

And what about the personalities of the students? We measured their levels of the HEXACO factors by self-report and also by observer report from their friends or roommates or romantic partners. Of the students who were most willing to profit at the expense of the public good, about three-quarters were below average in H; by contrast, of the students who were *least* willing, about three-quarters were above average in H.[3]

Perhaps these results overestimate the number of students who would make the unethical business decisions. After all, the situations were hypothetical, without any real risks of public harm or of criminal prosecution. But then again, the situations also lacked real money, so perhaps in a real-life situation even more of the students would put money over morality.

Unethical corporate activity is one way that low-H people express their personalities in today's market economy. But to some extent, the market economy actually constrains the selfishness of low-H people, because most of them can satisfy their greed only by producing things that others want. When law enforcement is good enough that crime generally doesn't pay, and when people can freely exchange labour and property, the only reliable way to get rich is to provide a good or a service that others will buy. As Adam Smith put it, "It is not from the benevolence of the butcher, the brewer, or the baker that we expect our dinner, but from their regard to their own self-interest."[4] The beauty of Smith's free market, at least in principle, is that the would-be thief and the would-be overlord must work for a living, perhaps in the food processing industry.

Yet low-H people find ways to defeat the spirit, and even the letter, of the rules that govern a market economy. The essence of the low-H personality is a willingness to gain by exploiting others, and therefore such people will always be ready to cheat in their economic transactions, with greater or lesser degrees of subtlety.

Anyone who sells on the principle "Let the buyer beware" is following the low-H strategy of doing business. Think of the stereotype of the used-car salesman or the shady building contractor. Similarly, anyone who tricks people into making ill-advised deals is using a classic low-H tactic. One excellent example is predatory lending, where the lender's aim is to foreclose on the assets of a borrower who probably will be unable to repay a loan. (So too is borrowing under false pretences, for example, by exaggerating income on a loan application or by planning simply to walk away if unable to repay the loan.) Yet another tactic of low-H persons involves shifting costs onto third parties so that the public must pay the "externalities" associated with their business. Classic cases here are the business owner who dumps toxic waste or who sells addictive drugs or deadly weapons.

Tax evasion is another means by which low-H people under-mine the market economy. Tax rates differ from one jurisdiction to the next, but every society must raise some taxes to pay for the public goods that its people deem important. Low-H people are disproportionately those who evade their taxes or avoid them in ways that are legal but contrary to the spirit of the laws. For example, income tax laws in many countries generally allow a var-iety of exemptions and deductions. Some of these are obvious and are claimed by virtually everyone, but others are obscure loop-holes that are discovered only by people who actively search for them. This means that the burden of paying taxes is shifted from people who try to avoid paying them onto people who don't. This essentially means that high-H persons—those whose sense of social responsibility outweighs their greed—end up subsidiz-ing low-H persons. (There are some high-H people who openly refuse to pay taxes on the grounds that the money would be used for immoral purposes, such as subsidizing aggressive wars. But we doubt that many of the tax-dodging crowd are taking their inspir-ation from Thoreau or Gandhi.) And the free riding of low-H persons isn't limited to tax evasion: it is people who are low in H who would claim benefits they don't really deserve, as in cases of welfare fraud or disability insurance fraud.

BOX 9–2   The H Factor and the Free Rider Problem

A recent study from Germany neatly illustrates the problem of free riding in low-H persons. Researchers Benjamin Hilbig, Ingo Zettler, and Timo Heydasch examined people's behaviour in a "public goods game."[5] In this game, each person is given an initial endowment of points, and each person can contribute any number of his or her points to a common pool. All points contributed to the common pool are multiplied and then distributed equally among all of the persons—regardless of each person's contribution.

Notice that the best outcome for the group collectively is for everyone to contribute heavily to the common pool. However, for any given person there is the temptation to be a free rider— to keep one's points and then benefit from everyone else's contributions. In this way, this public goods game captures the essence of many real-life situations, such as paying one's taxes, refraining from littering, paying the fare on public transit, and refraining from watering one's lawn during a drought.

Hilbig, Zettler, and Heydasch found that people who were very low in H contributed a little more than 30% of their points on average, whereas people who were very high in H contributed almost 70% of their points on average. Using these results, the researchers calculated what would happen in a group consisting (a) only of persons above average in H, and (b) only of persons below average in H. In a group of five high-H people, the total gain for the whole group would be about 25% higher than in a group of five low-H people.

It's easy to see that a community of high-H people would function much more effectively than would a community of low-H people. For some speculation about how an entire society of high-H persons might look, see Box 9–3.

Even when low-H people conform perfectly to the ideals of the market economy, they can still do a lot of harm. Consider conspicuous consumption, which is one of the hallmarks of the low-H personality. At first regard, this might not seem to be a major social problem: If low-H people want to waste their money on expensive, flashy toys, well, who cares? But conspicuous consumption by some has harmful consequences for all.

The economist Robert H. Frank has explained the problem as follows.[6] First, people try to outspend others on certain kinds of goods, simply so that they can have better—and be *seen* to have better—than other people do. For example, people like to have the nicest car or house or clothes or jewellery or furniture or restaurant reservations. In contrast, they don't compete in this way when spending money on, say, their insurance policies. This produces an expenditure arms race, in which people spend more and more money on these so-called positional goods. To get that money, people may take on large debts and may sacrifice much of their leisure time; they may also demand reductions in taxes— taxes that could be spent on public goods such as roads or schools or hospitals. But this escalation of spending doesn't make people any happier, because each person's relative standing in the competition of consumption remains more or less the same: on average, we never actually overtake the Joneses.

Now, if high-H people could just exempt themselves from this competition altogether, they could avoid many of its negative effects. But they can't. When low-H people create a speculative bubble (such as the real estate bubbles of the 2000s), the result is an economic crisis that causes unemployment for low-H and high-H people alike. And the arms race for luxury goods will cause most high-H people to spend more money even though they don't care about showing off. For example, when low-H people buy ever larger cars in an effort to show off, high-H people who would prefer to buy smaller cars feel at higher risk of being killed in a car accident and may feel compelled to upsize. Or when low-H people spend extravagantly on, say, business suits, high-H people who would rather just buy a basic suit may find themselves being taken less seriously at job interviews, making them feel compelled to follow the mantra of "dress for success."

Power

When Lord Acton said that power corrupts, he missed half the story: power also *attracts* the corrupt. Low-H people crave power, and they express this in a variety of attitudes. Consider the simple statement, "I would like to have more power than other people," which Lew Goldberg included in a questionnaire that he gave to his sample of Oregon adults. Among people who strongly disagreed with that statement, the large majority (over 80%) were above average in the H factor; among people who agreed or strongly agreed, most (again over 80%) were below average in the H factor.

Other links between low H and the need for power over others emerged from this sample of Oregon adults. Goldberg administered the Campbell Interest and Skill Survey, which assesses people's interests in various occupations and indicates how closely their responses match those of workers in those occupations. For example, if the pattern of your responses on the survey is similar to that of accountants, then you will score highly on the "Accountants" scale. There are 59 such occupations in this survey, and of those 59, the "CEO/President" scale was the one that showed the strongest link with low levels of the H factor (a correlation of about −.35). This meant that even though many CEOs and presidents are highly ethical people, the average CEO or president apparently has interests similar to those of low-H people.

Probably the central problem of human society is that the people who most want power—people low in H—are also the people most likely to abuse it. Democracy and limited government can go a long way toward solving this problem. In a democracy, you can gain power only by making some credible promises to give voters things they want, and you can keep power only by persuading voters that you have delivered on those promises. And in any system of limited government, you can have only so much power, because other branches and levels of government will act as checks against you.

But even in countries that enjoy democratic and limited government, low-H people can gain power by deceit and then abuse that power. When seeking power, skilled politicians will successfully mislead voters, and deception in politics is less strictly regulated than is deception in the marketplace. For example, advertising by political candidates generally isn't subject to the laws that govern commercial advertising, and promises by political candidates generally aren't treated as formal contracts. In fact, a total avoidance of deception can be fatal to success in politics: a politician who tells people what they don't want to hear will probably not last long.

Once ensconced in office, politicians—and the public servants who carry out their policies—can use their power to personal advantage, as far as they can get away with doing so. Even the least corrupt countries have occasional scandals when politicians and other government officials are caught taking bribes or kickbacks or awarding contracts to their cronies. Another variant is the misuse of public funds, as when politicians or bureaucrats claim extravagant amounts for expenses that are personal rather than professional. (Of course, this also happens in the private sector, and sometimes too in not-for-profit organizations.)

But the abuse of power by political leaders and government officials is hardly limited to personal corruption. The most spectacular—and terrifying—abuses are those involving aggressive war and other forms of mass murder. When low-H persons attain positions of essentially unchecked power, and when those persons are motivated by some ideology, the consequences are often horrific. In the most extreme cases—think of Hitler or Stalin—the toll may be counted in the tens of millions of innocent lives.

Let's turn now to power on a much pettier scale. In modern societies, economic power is diffused throughout the private sector rather than concentrated solely in government. In corporations spanning the range of economic activity, many low-H workers jockey for position, hoping to ascend the corporate ladder by whatever means will succeed. Just as a politician will tell voters what they want to hear, many employees will be yes-men and yes-women, cynically currying favour with their supervisors and other bosses in the hope of rising through the corporate ranks. But the

tactics used by low-H employees to get ahead at work are not limited to yea-saying and flattery (recall our discussion of workplace
impression management in Chapter 5). They also practise a much
wider array of Machiavellian tactics. Some of them claim credit
for achievements that were really due—at least in large part—to
the effort and talent of others. And some go even further, seeking to damage the reputations of co-workers by criticizing their
work unjustly or by spreading unflattering rumours about them,
whether true or not. And a few will go so far as to threaten and
intimidate their current or prospective rivals.

All of these examples of Machiavellian tactics in the workplace
have their counterparts in schools, from the primary grades right
up to university classes. In some cases the goal is to gain favour
with teachers, but the main preoccupation for most students is
their status with their peers. And here the young low-H person
may find much opportunity for bullying others,[7] whether by overt
physical intimidation (of the kind typically favoured by boys) or
by more subtle arts of social exclusion (which are perhaps practised
more skilfully by girls than by boys, who nonetheless get a lot of
practice). For very low-H people, social relationships are a zero sum
game in which all tactics are justified in the battle to attain status.

Sex

Sex is a domain in which people give each other much pleasure,
but it's also one in which people exploit each other quite ruth-
lessly. Modern countries generally have laws that limit the worst of
the sexual exploitation that some low-H people would be tempted
to commit, such as sexual assaults or sexual abuse of children. But

low H is also involved in other, subcriminal forms of exploitation in sexual relationships.

Consider the cad philosophy of "love them and leave them" (or its less euphemistic equivalent involving words that start with "f"). In this familiar story, one person, almost always a man, uses false affection or false promises to obtain sexual favours from another person, almost always a woman. He pretends to love her simply so that she will let him have sex with her. This is classic low-H behaviour, and at least under some conditions, it would serve to propagate low-H tendencies into the next generation: the successful Don Juan might end up as the biological father of many children by many mothers, without actually raising those children or providing for them in any way.

A different kind of exploitation by low-H men is that of polygyny, whereby some men have more than one wife and other men remain unmarried. Note that even though the status of women in polygynous societies is generally rather low, not all women are opposed to polygyny. To paraphrase George Bernard Shaw, a woman might prefer a one-tenth share of a first-rate man to a full share of a third-rate man, if we assume that the men who acquire multiple wives are "first-rate" by definition. However, polygyny is grossly exploitive of the men in polygynous societies who—for whatever reason—are unable to marry. In a polygynous society, many men have little prospect of having a wife and children and thus of having any family life. This isn't to say that the men who do attain multiple wives must be low in H, but it's a fair bet that low-H men are those who are most supportive of such a system. (Recall from Chapter 7 that people who favour social hierarchies tend to be low in H.)

Another form of exploitation is that of cheating on a romantic partner with whom one is supposed to have a monogamous relationship. People low in H—men or women—will not be much deterred from infidelity by an ethical reluctance to betray the trust of their spouse. If the opportunity comes along to have an affair with someone sexier—either more physically attractive or of higher status—the low-H person will likely take it. This isn't to say that the correspondence between low H and infidelity is perfect: some low-H people will simply not be much interested in extramarital affairs, or will be too wary of the reaction of a vigilant and suspicious spouse; and a few high-H people will have affairs if their spouse is sufficiently unkind or if their marriage is sufficiently unhappy. But for very low-H people, the default setting is a willingness to cheat on their spouse.

Sexual histories tend to differ between low-H people and high-H people, especially among men. Low-H people pursue more short-term relationships, make more attempts to poach other people's partners, and have more sex partners than do high-H people. In one of our studies, we asked university students to indicate how many different sex partners they realistically foresaw themselves having during the next five years. About 10% of male students indicated nine or more partners, and about three-quarters of those students scored below the average of the H factor.[8] None of the other personality factors was a better predictor than H of the expected number of sex partners. This doesn't mean that the low-H men would necessarily end up with more sex partners, although we expect that to some extent they would. But the fact that they expect—and presumably want to have—more partners is itself interesting.

As we mentioned above, it's mostly men—low-H men—who adopt the classic cad pattern of using insincere affection as a means to gaining sexual gratification. Perhaps the female equivalent of the cad is the tease: a woman who holds out the false prospect of a sexual relationship with a man in order to obtain from him favours of various kinds—gifts of money or jewellery, help with work at school or the office, and so on. For women low in H, sex and affection are tools for manipulating men into giving them what they want. Another incarnation of the low-H woman is the gold digger, who seeks to marry simply with a view to obtaining the wealth and status of her prospective husband, either with or without the plan to divorce him later. For women low in H (and especially those who are also low in E), the idea of marrying for love seems ridiculously naive, and the idea of marrying for money is simply common sense.

Low H also plays an important role in sexual harassment of the quid pro quo variety. In the typical sexual quid pro quo, a person in a position of authority, usually a man, obtains sexual favours from a person having less power, usually a woman, in exchange for some reward, such as a raise or a promotion. Sometimes the "reward" is simply the avoidance of some penalty, such as being fired.

In one of our research projects, we compared the personalities of people who would engage in quid pro quo sexual harassment with those of people who wouldn't.[9] In studying this question, we wanted to examine both "sides" of the quid pro quo equation: What are the personality traits of people who would offer rewards in exchange for sexual favours? And what are the personality traits of people who would grant—or even offer—sexual favours in exchange for rewards?

To find out, we asked our research participants—men and women university students—to consider two pairs of related scenarios. Here's one of the two pairs:

Suppose that you are a high-level government official. You are currently making decisions about the awarding of a major government contract, and there are several companies that are competing for this contract. You are very strongly attracted to the representative of one of these companies, and this person seems to be very strongly motivated to get the contract (which would mean a large commission for that representative). In fact, you are sure that this person would perform sexual favours in exchange for a major government contract, and you are also sure that you would not be caught or punished in any way for making this arrangement.

Would you give this representative the contract in exchange for sexual favours?

(1) Definitely No   (2) Probably Not

(3) Probably Yes   (4) Definitely Yes

Now imagine a situation similar to the one above, but suppose instead that you are a company representative instead of a government official. Assume that you could definitely receive the contract and commission in exchange for sexual favours, and that no one would find out about this exchange.

Would you be willing to provide sexual favours in exchange for the contract?

(1) Definitely Not   (2) Probably Not

(3) Probably Yes   (4) Definitely Yes

As you can see, the first scenario assesses the willingness to trade rewards for sexual favours, and the second assesses the converse. Notice that there is no suggestion of any desperate circumstances facing the company representative: what we wanted to measure was the willingness to trade sexual favours for some substantial reward even when one's basic needs are securely being met. (We realized that a person who normally would never seek advantage through sexual favours might submit to a sexual quid pro quo if there seemed to be no other choice: consider, for example, a single mother faced with the prospect of losing her job.)

How many of our participants indicated a willingness to make these sexual quid pro quos? Only a minority, but a fairly substantial minority. For each scenario in the pair given above, about three-quarters of women and about one-half of men responded "definitely not"; fewer than 10% of women and about 20% of men responded "probably yes" or "definitely yes." Men were thus more receptive to the idea of sexual quid pro quos than women were.

This result wasn't surprising, but an unexpected finding was that the two scenarios hardly differed in their pattern of responses. We had expected men to be relatively more willing to trade material rewards for sexual favours, and we had expected women to be relatively more willing to trade sexual favours for material rewards. However, there was little evidence of this except that women were slightly more willing to give a yes response to the second scenario than to the first.

What were the differences in personality between the people who were willing to make sexual quid pro quos, and those who weren't? The biggest difference was in the H factor: of the people who definitely wouldn't do any of the sexual quid pro quos, only about one-third were below the average level of H. But of the people who probably would do the sexual quid pro quos, more than three-quarters were below that average level. None of the other HEXACO factors showed any differences nearly as large as this one. Of the six personality dimensions, it's H that best predicts the likelihood of seeking a sexual quid pro quo.

BOX 9–3   Hutopia?

Imagine a society in which many people are very high in H and hardly any people are low. What would such a society look like? We can speculate on this question by extrapolating from the characteristics of higher- and lower-H people and from their responses to questions about their attitudes on political issues.

First, it would be free and democratic. People who are high in H aren't power hungry, and they wouldn't want megalomaniacs for leaders. In a high-H society, civil liberties would be strong and the powers of government would be dispersed widely across its various levels (i.e., federal, state/provincial, local) and branches (i.e., executive, legislative, judicial). Corruption among politicians and civil servants would be extremely rare.

Second, it would be egalitarian. High-H individuals avoid materialism and conspicuous consumption and dislike social hierarchies. Accordingly, a high-H society would have a rather small gap between the "rich" and the "poor." For example, the salaries of CEOs would be only several times those of the average workers in their companies—not several dozen or several hundred times higher. Also, with very little "free riding" in a high-H society, taxpayers would willingly support an extensive system of universal social welfare programs, such as direct government payments to poor households and unemployed persons, as well as publicly funded health care, education, and old-age pensions. These programs would be funded through rather high taxes levied chiefly on excess consumption rather than on income or on capital.[10]

Third, it would be ethically strict. High-H people have high standards as to what constitutes ethical behaviour, and this would be reflected in the laws of a high-H society. Such a society would set a low threshold for regulating or criminalizing any activities that exploit individuals or impose negative externalities on the broader society. For example, it would have strict controls on pollution, addictive drugs, gambling, weapons, dangerous products (both physical and financial), and animal exploitation. In a high-H society, concerns about exploitation and negative externalities would often outweigh concerns about nanny-state regulation. Attitudes toward sexual behaviour wouldn't necessarily be prudish, but concerns about exploitation would likely mean some very sharp limits on pornography and prostitution. Laws against the classic common crimes—the use of force or fraud—would also be strictly enforced. (But note that strict enforcement doesn't imply arbitrary police powers or brutal punishments, neither of which would appeal to the people of a high-H society.)

Fourth, it would be benevolent: high-H people want to cooperate rather than dominate, and a society of such people would give considerable humanitarian and development aid without trying to impose its will on others. A high-H society would be inclined toward pacifism, yet it would have a strong potential for self-defence, given the high level of trust and cohesion among its citizens. Still, the high-H society might be a victim of its own success: its high quality of life would likely attract not only high-H immigrants but low-H immigrants as well.

As you can see from our tour through the domains of money, power, and sex, dealing with low-H people is often unpleasant at best. In the next chapter, we'll have some advice for identifying low-H people and for steering around them.

HOW TO IDENTIFY LOW-H PEOPLE—
AND HOW TO LIVE AROUND THEM

To be able to identify low-H people is a useful skill. If you know who they are, you're better equipped to avoid being exploited by them, whether in the next few minutes or many years down the road. Fortunately, some of the traits that indicate low H aren't obviously undesirable, which means that low-H people won't necessarily even try to conceal those aspects of their personalities.

If you want a really accurate idea of a person's level of H, you will need to observe the whole array of H-related traits as expressed in diverse situations and on many occasions. Only by observing a wide range of the person's behaviour, and appreciating the various contexts in which it occurs, can you have any justified confidence in your assessment. Your first impressions might be mistaken, and it's easy to misdiagnose someone on the basis of a couple of isolated, ambiguous observations, particularly if you're starting with some prejudice (whether positive or negative) toward that person. Having said this, there will be many situations where you don't have the luxury of time and where your main motive is to avoid being exploited. In those cases it's better to use what information you have and to err on the side of underestimating the person's level of H.

In this chapter, we discuss some signs that can help you identify low-H people, and we offer some advice for living in a world that contains quite a few of them. But first, we should mention some signs that you might *think* would mean a person is high in H—but actually don't.

Not-So-Valid Signs of High H

Respectability

The link between respectability and the H factor is easy to overestimate. Many people assume that a well-spoken, well-dressed, and well-mannered person must also be well intentioned. These outward signs of respectability probably do indicate a reasonable level of self-control—here is someone who at least understands and can conform to what society considers desirable behaviour. Conversely, if someone is foul-mouthed and rude and generally scary, that's obviously not a good sign. The problem is that many low-H persons indeed have that reasonable level of self-control (recall Chapter 4). And some low-H people find that by appearing to be well socialized, it's much easier to take advantage of others. (It's harder to cheat people effectively if you look shady to them.) A respectable appearance is not a sure indication of trustworthiness.

It's equally unwise to take it for granted that every respectable position in society is occupied by a high-H person. If someone has a respected occupation, a prominent role in their community, and a regular place at religious services, we can again infer that this person probably has a certain amount of self-control. But here the same point applies: many low-H people can navigate social relationships quite successfully, and many low-H people aspire to a position of high status.

Anti-Conformity

Perhaps the flip side of respectability is anti-conformity. By this we mean a calculated effort to be visibly different from others and to bring attention to one's defiance of convention. (This anti-conformity contrasts with the more natural nonconformity of people who happen to be different simply by being themselves.) For example, people who have an unusual style of dress might simply be expressing their personal taste—or they might be acting affectedly in an effort to appear special. The point is that anti-conformity isn't the same thing as authenticity and doesn't necessarily indicate a high level of H.

Religious Piety

As we explained in Chapter 8, genuinely religious people tend to be somewhat high in H. But some people who publicly display their religiosity, such as by attending religious services or participating in religious rituals, are low-H people who are simply aiming to create an image of respectability and to maintain status within their community. The bottom line is that outward signs of religious commitment aren't a dependable indicator of a high-H personality.

Championing the Underdog

Some people vocally defend the disadvantaged and the oppressed, and many of those people are motivated by a sincere desire to promote social justice. But for some of these champions of the underdog, this role serves merely as a vehicle for obtaining a position of high status. When you see a prominent defender of the downtrodden, it isn't immediately obvious whether that person is a high-H idealist or a low-H opportunist.

Blunt Criticism

When people criticize, they sometimes sandwich their criticism between slices of self-professed honesty: "I'll be honest with you … [insert rather hurtful summary of shortcomings here]. I'm just being honest." Now, sometimes this criticism may be justified; it may even be constructive and meant genuinely for the good of its recipient. But some people use the being-honest gambit to make a virtue of their habit of delivering harsh comments. Having a low threshold for criticizing others is not normally an indication of high H. Instead, it's generally an expression of low A and may even suggest a *low* level of H, particularly if the intent is really to undermine the listener's self-esteem or their esteem for a third party.

Publicly Displayed Generosity

On the surface, people who give their wealth away to some worthy cause would seem clearly to be high-H people. But this isn't necessarily so. Instead, it depends a lot on whether the acts of philanthropy are intended for public display. If the donation is highly visible, being made amid great fanfare and ceremony, then there is no need to invoke a high level of H as a cause of the generosity. Instead, the gift is more accurately viewed as a kind of informal exchange of money for social status. Consider a wealthy person who has more than enough money to enjoy a luxurious lifestyle, but who lacks the esteem and respect of other prominent people. A major donation to (say) a hospital or a university or a museum or a park will attract a lot of positive attention from the media, from politicians, and from the general public. Thus, even among wealthy people who happen to be low in H, we can expect a great deal of high-profile philanthropy.

In fact, some people who are very low in H are also highly enthusiastic contributors to charity. You can probably recall at least some cases of people who advertise themselves as philanthropists, but have also been criminally convicted, usually for white-collar offences. (If you can't remember any such cases, try searching the Internet with the keywords "philanthropist" and "convicted".)

Philanthropic acts are much more likely to reflect a high level of H when the donor gives without seeking any attention. Donations made anonymously, or with instructions not to reveal the identity of the donor, are much more consistent with the outlook of high-H persons, because the gift is a genuine act of altruism rather than simply a purchase of social status.

This doesn't mean that high-profile philanthropy is a sign that the donor has a *low* level of H. Some wealthy high-H people might feel a certain degree of social pressure to donate money, and they might want to make some publicly visible gifts in order to relieve that pressure, beyond any gifts that they might make (or might prefer to make) privately.

Even when publicly displayed generosity might not be motivated by a high level of H, it can still be beneficial to society. The very fact that social status must be purchased by making worthwhile gifts to the public good is encouraging, as it suggests that low-H people must play nice in order to have the respect they crave; they can't simply bully or threaten us all. But then again, if the wealth of the low-H pseudo-philanthropist has been gained dishonestly, the net effect on society will still be negative.

Valid Signs of Low H

Beating the System

It might seem obvious that you shouldn't trust people who tell you—without joking—about various ways of breaking the law. But some people who brag about how to beat the system—for example, by evading income taxes or customs duties, or by stealing from businesses—may come across as roguishly charming and harmless. And they may rationalize their actions as being not really wrong, because no single person is directly harmed to any significant extent. Don't be fooled: people who will cheat an institution will likely cheat individuals too, and that includes you.

Instrumental Ingratiation

Some people can be very friendly and polite and pleasant—but mainly toward people who have something they want, or who hold some position of influence. Sometimes you can observe this as a third party: consider the player who is attentive to a prospective conquest until he has sex with her, or the politician who is the best friend of whichever interest group must be courted next. It can sometimes be more difficult to discern this kind of ingratiation, as we saw in the study of co-workers in Chapter 5: unless you know a person very well, it isn't easy to distinguish flattery from sincere respect, or affectation from genuine politeness. The point is simply that people who are selectively nice, reserving their affection and compliments for those who are or will be useful to them, are not likely to be loyal friends.

Some low-H individuals say that people who don't act in this way are simply being naive, but in most cases this claim simply reflects their own cynicism. Many people are well aware that they could use false ingratiation as a way of getting what they want, and may even feel tempted to do so, but decline as a matter of principle to use such tactics. Apart from really dictatorial settings, where one's welfare may really depend on the whims of powerful people, the use of ingratiation tactics is largely a function of a low-H personality.

Gambling and Financial Speculation

Gamblers tend to be low in H. More precisely, people who often bet a lot of money—at casinos, on sports events, in card games, or whatever—usually have a low level of H, often combined with a low level of E. (People who become addicted to gambling are probably also low in C.)[1] The same applies to people whose financial investments amount to short-term speculation, whether on currencies or commodities or real estate or stocks. Of course, many high-H persons will buy a weekly lottery ticket or play some low-stakes poker, and many high-H persons will invest money in business ventures that have a real risk of failure. But people who regularly risk a lot of money in gambling or speculation probably have a strong desire to get rich quickly or to get something for nothing. Such people tend to be low in the H factor, so it's best not to be too trusting of them.

Sexual Infidelity

As we noted in Chapter 9, people who cheat on their romantic partners tend to be low in H, and the same is true of people who try to poach the partners of others. Although such persons will often find it wise to be subtle or sneaky in their behaviour, many of them are quite happy to express their cynical outlook on sexual relationships. Moreover, a low-H man is likely to boast about his sexual conquests, and a low-H woman is likely to boast about the material benefits of her relationships or the status of her partners. The point is that people who are sexually unfaithful to their partners, or who take an instrumental approach to sexual relationships, are likely to be low in the H factor.

Conspicuous Consumption (and Name Dropping)

A person who displays wealth ostentatiously is trying to signal that he or she is an important, high-status person. But what conspicuous consumption really signals is a low level of the H factor. Materialistic and ostentatious people tend to be selfish, deceitful, and insincere: people who want more than their share generally feel entitled to have more than their share, and they're willing to take it by force or by fraud, if they judge that they will succeed in doing so. So when someone shows off a lot of expensive things— home, car, clothing, jewellery, food, drinks—you should be wary of getting into any business or romantic relationships with that person. The same goes for someone who is readily impressed with such displays and who aspires to match them.

Keep in mind that what matters here is the overall *pattern* of conspicuous consumption, not merely an isolated extravagance or two. For example, a high-H birdwatcher might own an expensive pair of binoculars, a high-H antiques fan might own an expensive old table, and a high-H car enthusiast might own an expensive automobile. But in those cases, the person probably appreciates the item for its intrinsic qualities rather than for its ability to impress other people. In contrast, it's very unlikely that someone would own (or aspire to own) a wide variety of highly visible luxury items out of some intrinsic interest in each of those particular items. Most people who display many different kinds of expensive items are expressing a low level of H.

Low-H people sometimes defend greed on the grounds that it motivates hard work and innovation, thereby driving economic progress. (Recall the "greed is good" speech in the 1980s movie *Wall Street*.) Now, it's true that people—even high-H people—generally prefer having more wealth and status rather than less, and that people are less likely to work hard and innovate if there is little reward for productivity. But this doesn't mean that the greediest people—those who most desire money and luxury and power—will be particularly diligent or creative. On the contrary, the consistent finding in personality structure research is that materialistic, social-climbing people are no more hard-working or innovative than everyone else. What's more, greedy people will try to get something for nothing: if they judge that they can get away with it, they're happy to sell you things you don't need, to sell you things that don't work, and even to sell you things that could kill either you or the worker who made them.

Name dropping is analogous to conspicuous consumption, but the objects of display are social affiliations rather than material goods. Some people will bring your attention to their relationships with famous people or their memberships in prestigious institutions. Think of the person who displays photographs of himself or herself with celebrities or politicians, or who tells you all about his or her connections with those persons.

"Above the Law" Mentality

Some people decide that they belong to a special class of persons to whom the normal rules should not apply. Their self-appointed membership in this elite may be based on their social class or ethnicity, or on what they perceive to be their own superiority of intellect, or attractiveness, or athleticism, or talent, or any other asset. Depending on your own position in the pecking order as they see it (or as they would have you think they see it), they may assure you that you, too, belong to this elite. Don't be seduced by this. When people see themselves as Nietzschean supermen and superwomen who should be exempt from the laws and norms that govern lesser beings, they will also feel quite justified in exploiting the latter in one way or another. You can see this when a high-ranking bureaucrat puts extravagant spending on the government's tab, or when the board of directors awards its members a bonus at investors' expense. But you also see this when wealthy or famous or high-ranking people are caught shoplifting (yes, shoplifting): they simply feel entitled to take without paying.

Incidentally, the self-appointed supermen and superwomen generally aren't any more super than the rest of us. Even if we put aside their rather less-than-super approach to personal ethics, there is not much that is impressive about people who have a strong sense of entitlement: on average, they aren't any tougher or prettier or smarter, and they don't have any more talent or (genuine) charm. The low-H person tends to claim any of his or her personal strengths as proof of entitlement; the high-H person doesn't.

By the way, don't confuse this low-H attitude of entitlement with mere overconfidence. Some people are inclined to overestimate their abilities or attributes—say, their intelligence or athleticism or attractiveness—without seeing themselves as deserving of special status. By contrast, low-H people do see themselves as superior beings, but they don't necessarily overestimate their own level of any particular asset.

Contempt of Other Groups

People who are high in H don't necessarily believe that all human groups are equal in every observable characteristic. But high-H people generally do believe that people of every group are deserving of dignity and fair treatment. Thus, when some people take delight in making disparaging comments about other groups, this is a sign of low H. For example, low-H people are more likely than high-H people to make ethnic jokes of any but the most good-natured variety. They're also more likely to mock other groups or to make dehumanizing comments about them.

Living Around Low-H People

What should you do when you realize that someone is probably very low in H? First of all, don't get carried away. It's probably not a good idea to proclaim your diagnosis to others. And it's definitely not a good idea to undertake any vigilante-style action against that person.

The best advice is simply to limit your interaction with people who are low in H. Don't choose them as romantic partners. Don't choose them as business partners. Don't even choose them as tennis partners, or as bridge partners. Just stay away from them.

Now, if you're a low-H person yourself, it's not obvious what advice we should give you. On the one hand, high-H people won't try to take advantage of you in the way that low-H people will, so you might be better off seeking the company of high-H people. On the other hand, you'll much prefer the approach that your fellow low-H people take in dealing with the world. Probably your best bet is to figure out which low-H people would make the most effective allies in your quest for money and power, and then team up with them. Just be sure to watch them very carefully.

What if you're already in close contact with a low-H person, either professionally or personally, and can't easily get away? Don't fool yourself into thinking that you can somehow teach a low-H person to appreciate the joys of being fair for the sake of fairness. The better approach is to find ways of aligning your interests with their interests, so that they get what they want by doing what you want. But we realize that it's easier to say this than to do it, and the challenge is that the low-H person will always be alert to ways of exploiting you. Fortunately, the most serious forms of exploitation are recognized as crimes, so in the worst situations you should go to the police. As we discussed in Chapter 4, however, low-H people vary a great deal in their potential for really criminal, predatory behaviour, depending on their levels of the other personality dimensions. For example, a low-H person who is high in A, C, and E will probably be rather annoying, but he or she is much less likely to be a psychopathic or dangerous person than is someone who combines low levels of these traits with low H.

The flip side of avoiding low-H people is seeking out high-H people. As we explained in Chapter 6, people tend to form most of their close relationships with those who have similar levels of H and hence have similar values and world views. People generally aren't even aware of this tendency, but if you're a high-H person, you can make a conscious choice to associate with other high-H people. This strategy also applies to places: when deciding where to work or where to live, you can seek out organizations and communities that share the values of high-H people. By gaining the benefits of cooperation with one another, high-H persons can thrive in what often seems like a low-H world.

Epilogue

ON BECOMING A HIGH-H PERSON

The two of us have been studying the H factor since the late 1990s, and most of the time we treat it simply as a topic of scientific study. But our work on the H factor has made us more aware of our own behaviour. Each of us can look back on his life and recall having acted in some decidedly low-H ways. Although it doesn't feel good to think about those occasions, it does at least make us think about how we ought to act in the future. Already, each of us has often behaved a bit differently after considering how a high-H person would approach a given situation. We haven't achieved anything remotely approaching perfection in this regard, but we do find ourselves trying to be more straightforward and less self-important, more ethical and less materialistic.

Our own cases help show an important point about the H factor: your level of H doesn't just depend on your genes and on your childhood—it also depends on your own free will. We assume that by nature you're fairly high in H, given that you've already read nearly this whole book. (Most really low-H persons would be turned off long before reaching this chapter.) Now, if we're right—if you're a somewhat high-H person by nature—then you'll very likely accept that being a high-H person is a good thing: you'll believe that being sincere and modest is inherently better than being deceitful and conceited. But unless you're at the extreme high end of the H dimension, you probably feel at least some low-H motivations: maybe you sometimes manipulate others a bit, or give a little less than you really should, or try to impress others with your status.

Well, if you really do want to be higher in H, you can use your high-H idealism to overcome your low-H inclinations. Even though you have some temptations to deceive or dominate or exploit other people, you can decide to be alert to those temptations and then to resist them. In trying to be higher in H, you might even find it useful to follow some specific set of prescriptions, whether secular or religious (recall the "Quaker testimonies" of Chapter 8). Of course, this kind of conscious choice won't change your "natural" level of H as given by your genes and early experiences. But who cares? Your actual level of H will be higher just the same. Only you will know the difference, and this is surely one case where no one will mind being deceived.

THE HEXACO PERSONALITY INVENTORY—REVISED

The HEXACO Personality Inventory–Revised (HEXACO–PI–R) assesses the six major personality factors discussed in Chapters 3 and 4. In this Appendix, we provide the short (60-item) version of the HEXACO–PI–R in both self-report and observer report forms. At the end of the Appendix, we provide instructions for scoring and interpreting your responses.

HEXACO Personality Inventory—Revised (Self-Report Form)*

On the following pages is a series of statements about you. Please read each statement and decide how much you agree or disagree with that statement, using the following scale. Then write your response in the corresponding space on the answer sheet on page 177. (Write your responses in the spaces next to the numbers, not in the spaces between parentheses.) Please answer every statement, even if you are not completely sure of your response.

* HEXACO Personality Inventory—Revised (Self-Report Form) © Kibeom Lee and Michael C. Ashton

1 = strongly disagree   2 = disagree   3 = neutral
4 = agree   5 = strongly agree

1. I would be quite bored by a visit to an art gallery.
2. I plan ahead and organize things, to avoid scrambling at the last minute.
3. I rarely hold a grudge, even against people who have badly wronged me.
4. I feel reasonably satisfied with myself overall.
5. I would feel afraid if I had to travel in bad weather conditions.
6. I wouldn't use flattery to get a raise or promotion at work, even if I thought it would succeed.
7. I'm interested in learning about the history and politics of other countries.
8. I often push myself very hard when trying to achieve a goal.
9. People sometimes tell me that I am too critical of others.
10. I rarely express my opinions in group meetings.
11. I sometimes can't help worrying about little things.
12. If I knew that I could never get caught, I would be willing to steal a million dollars.
13. I would enjoy creating a work of art, such as a novel, a song, or a painting.
14. When working on something, I don't pay much attention to small details.
15. People sometimes tell me that I'm too stubborn.
16. I prefer jobs that involve active social interaction to those that involve working alone.
17. When I suffer from a painful experience, I need someone to make me feel comfortable.

18. Having a lot of money is not especially important to me.
19. I think that paying attention to radical ideas is a waste of time.
20. I make decisions based on the feeling of the moment rather than on careful thought.
21. People think of me as someone who has a quick temper.
22. On most days, I feel cheerful and optimistic.
23. I feel like crying when I see other people crying.
24. I think that I am entitled to more respect than the average person is.
25. If I had the opportunity, I would like to attend a classical music concert.
26. When working, I sometimes have difficulties due to being disorganized.
27. My attitude toward people who have treated me badly is "forgive and forget."
28. I feel that I am an unpopular person.
29. When it comes to physical danger, I am very fearful.
30. If I want something from someone, I will laugh at that person's worst jokes.
31. I've never really enjoyed looking through an encyclopedia.
32. I do only the minimum amount of work needed to get by.
33. I tend to be lenient in judging other people.
34. In social situations, I'm usually the one who makes the first move.
35. I worry a lot less than most people do.
36. I would never accept a bribe, even if it were very large.
37. People have often told me that I have a good imagination.
38. I always try to be accurate in my work, even at the expense of time.

39. I am usually quite flexible in my opinions when people disagree with me.
40. The first thing that I always do in a new place is to make friends.
41. I can handle difficult situations without needing emotional support from anyone else.
42. I would get a lot of pleasure from owning expensive luxury goods.
43. I like people who have unconventional views.
44. I make a lot of mistakes because I don't think before I act.
45. Most people tend to get angry more quickly than I do.
46. Most people are more upbeat and dynamic than I generally am.
47. I feel strong emotions when someone close to me is going away for a long time.
48. I want people to know that I am an important person of high status.
49. I don't think of myself as the artistic or creative type.
50. People often call me a perfectionist.
51. Even when people make a lot of mistakes, I rarely say anything negative.
52. I sometimes feel that I am a worthless person.
53. Even in an emergency I wouldn't feel like panicking.
54. I wouldn't pretend to like someone just to get that person to do favours for me.
55. I find it boring to discuss philosophy.
56. I prefer to do whatever comes to mind, rather than stick to a plan.
57. When people tell me that I'm wrong, my first reaction is to argue with them.

58. When I'm in a group of people, I'm often the one who speaks on behalf of the group.
59. I remain unemotional even in situations where most people get very sentimental.
60. I'd be tempted to use counterfeit money, if I were sure I could get away with it.

HEXACO Personality Inventory—Revised (Observer Report Form)*

On the following pages is a series of statements about the person whose personality you would like to describe. Please read each statement and decide how much you agree or disagree with that statement, using the following scale. Then write your response in the corresponding space on the answer sheet on page 178. (Write your responses in the spaces next to the numbers on that page, not in the spaces between parentheses.) Please answer every statement, even if you are not completely sure of your response.

1 = strongly disagree	2 = disagree	3 = neutral
	4 = agree	5 = strongly agree

1. He/she would be quite bored by a visit to an art gallery.
2. He/she plans ahead and organizes things, to avoid scrambling at the last minute.
3. He/she rarely holds a grudge, even against people who have badly wronged him/her.
4. He/she feels reasonably satisfied with himself/herself overall.

* HEXACO Personality Inventory—Revised (Observer Report Form)
© Kibeom Lee and Michael C. Ashton

5. He/she would feel afraid if he/she had to travel in bad weather conditions.

6. He/she wouldn't use flattery to get a raise or promotion at work, even if he/she thought it would succeed.

7. He/she is interested in learning about the history and politics of other countries.

8. He/she often pushes himself/herself very hard when trying to achieve a goal.

9. People sometimes say that he/she is too critical of others.

10. He/she rarely expresses his/her opinions in group meetings.

11. He/she worries about little things.

12. If he/she knew that he/she could never get caught, he/she would be willing to steal a million dollars.

13. He/she would enjoy creating a work of art, such as a novel, a song, or a painting.

14. When working on something, he/she doesn't pay much attention to small details.

15. People sometimes think that he/she is too stubborn.

16. He/she prefers jobs that involve active social interaction to those that involve working alone.

17. When he/she suffers from a painful experience, he/she needs someone to make him/her feel comfortable.

18. Having a lot of money is not especially important to him/her.

19. He/she thinks that paying attention to radical ideas is a waste of time.

20. He/she makes decisions based on the feeling of the moment rather than on careful thought.

21. People think of him/her as someone who has a quick temper.

22. On most days, he/she feels cheerful and optimistic.

23. He/she feels like crying when he/she sees other people crying.

24. He/she thinks that he/she is entitled to more respect than the average person is.

25. If he/she had the opportunity, he/she would like to attend a classical music concert.

26. When working, he/she sometimes has difficulties due to being disorganized.

27. His/her attitude toward people who have treated him/her badly is "forgive and forget."

28. He/she feels that he/she is an unpopular person.

29. When it comes to physical danger, he/she is very fearful.

30. If he/she wants something from someone, he/she will laugh at that person's worst jokes.

31. He/she has never really enjoyed looking through an encyclopedia.

32. He/she does only the minimum amount of work needed to get by.

33. He/she tends to be lenient in judging other people.

34. In social situations, he/she is usually the one who makes the first move.

35. He/she worries a lot less than most people do.

36. He/she would never accept a bribe, even if it were very large.

37. He/she has a good imagination.

38. He/she always tries to be accurate in his/her work, even at the expense of time.

39. He/she is usually quite flexible in his/her opinions when people disagree with him/her.

40. The first thing that he/she always does in a new place is to make friends.
41. He/she can handle difficult situations without needing emotional support from anyone else.
42. He/she would get a lot of pleasure from owning expensive luxury goods.
43. He/she likes people who have unconventional views.
44. He/she makes a lot of mistakes because he/she doesn't think before he/she acts.
45. Most people tend to get angry more quickly than he/she does.
46. Most people are more upbeat and dynamic than he/she generally is.
47. He/she feels strong emotions when someone close to him/her is going away for a long time.
48. He/she wants people to know that he/she is an important person of high status.
49. I don't think of him/her as the artistic or creative type.
50. People often call him/her a perfectionist.
51. Even when people make a lot of mistakes, he/she rarely says anything negative.
52. He/she sometimes feels that he/she is a worthless person.
53. Even in an emergency he/she wouldn't feel like panicking.
54. He/she wouldn't pretend to like someone just to get that person to do favours for him/her.
55. He/she finds it boring to discuss philosophy.
56. He/she prefers to do whatever comes to mind, rather than stick to a plan.
57. When people tell him/her that he/she is wrong, his/her first reaction is to argue with them.

58. When he/she is in a group of people, he/she is often the one who speaks on behalf of the group.

59. He/she remains unemotional even in situations where most people get very sentimental.

60. He/she'd be tempted to use counterfeit money, if he/she were sure he/she could get away with it.

HEXACO-PI-R Scoring and Interpretation

To obtain accurate scores on the HEXACO–PI–R, please complete all of the steps below very carefully. Any errors may greatly distort your results!

1. Refer to the sheet containing responses to the HEXACO–PI–R (either self- or observer report). For all items WITHOUT an asterisk, please copy the response for each item into the adjacent space (i.e., between parentheses).

2. For all items WITH an asterisk, please recode the response for each item as follows, and then write the recoded response in the adjacent space (i.e., between parentheses).

   $1 \rightarrow 5$; $2 \rightarrow 4$; $3 \rightarrow 3$; $4 \rightarrow 2$; $5 \rightarrow 1$

3. After all of the spaces between parentheses have been filled appropriately, find the sum of all numbers in each of the six columns. Then recalculate each sum and resolve any errors.

4. These column sums represent your scores on six scales of this personality inventory. The scales, from left to right, are as follows:

> Openness to Experience (O)
> Conscientiousness (C)
> Agreeableness (A)
> Extraversion (X)
> Emotionality (E)
> Honesty-Humility (H)

5. To understand what these scales actually measure, see the descriptions in Table 3–1. This is important, because the scale names alone are not precise descriptions.

6. Use the following categories to interpret your scores. Note that "above average" is not necessarily better and that "below average" is not necessarily worse; recall the discussions of trade-offs in Chapter 3.

> Well above average: 44 or above
> Somewhat above average: 36 to 43
> About average: 28 to 35
> Somewhat below average: 20 to 27
> Well below average: 19 or below

7. Keep in mind that scores on this brief inventory are not perfect indications of personality trait levels. Although the HEXACO–PI–R is a well-validated personality inventory, the scores of any given person on a particular scale might overestimate or underestimate that person's true level of the personality dimension. For most people, the most accurate information about personality can be gained by considering self-reports in combination with observer reports from people who know that person well.

HEXACO-PI-R RESPONSE SHEET (Self-Report Form)

*1 __ (__)	2 __ (__)	3 __ (__)	4 __ (__)	5 __ (__)	6 __ (__)
7 __ (__)	8 __ (__)	*9 __ (__)	*10 __ (__)	11 __ (__)	*12 __ (__)
13 __ (__)	*14 __ (__)	*15 __ (__)	16 __ (__)	17 __ (__)	18 __ (__)
*19 __ (__)	*20 __ (__)	*21 __ (__)	22 __ (__)	23 __ (__)	*24 __ (__)
25 __ (__)	*26 __ (__)	27 __ (__)	*28 __ (__)	29 __ (__)	*30 __ (__)
*31 __ (__)	*32 __ (__)	33 __ (__)	34 __ (__)	*35 __ (__)	36 __ (__)
37 __ (__)	38 __ (__)	39 __ (__)	40 __ (__)	*41 __ (__)	*42 __ (__)
43 __ (__)	*44 __ (__)	45 __ (__)	*46 __ (__)	47 __ (__)	*48 __ (__)
*49 __ (__)	50 __ (__)	51 __ (__)	*52 __ (__)	*53 __ (__)	54 __ (__)
*55 __ (__)	*56 __ (__)	*57 __ (__)	58 __ (__)	*59 __ (__)	*60 __ (__)

SUM   __   __   __   __   __   __

HEXACO-PI-R RESPONSE SHEET (Observer Report Form)

*1 __ ( )	2 __ ( )	3 __ ( )	4 __ ( )	5 __ ( )	6 __ ( )
7 __ ( )	8 __ ( )	*9 __ ( )	*10 __ ( )	11 __ ( )	*12 __ ( )
13 __ ( )	*14 __ ( )	*15 __ ( )	16 __ ( )	17 __ ( )	18 __ ( )
*19 __ ( )	*20 __ ( )	*21 __ ( )	22 __ ( )	23 __ ( )	*24 __ ( )
25 __ ( )	*26 __ ( )	27 __ ( )	*28 __ ( )	29 __ ( )	*30 __ ( )
*31 __ ( )	*32 __ ( )	33 __ ( )	34 __ ( )	*35 __ ( )	36 __ ( )
37 __ ( )	38 __ ( )	39 __ ( )	40 __ ( )	*41 __ ( )	*42 __ ( )
43 __ ( )	*44 __ ( )	45 __ ( )	*46 __ ( )	47 __ ( )	*48 __ ( )
*49 __ ( )	50 __ ( )	51 __ ( )	*52 __ ( )	*53 __ ( )	54 __ ( )
*55 __ ( )	*56 __ ( )	*57 __ ( )	58 __ ( )	*59 __ ( )	*60 __ ( )
__	__	__	__	__	__

SUM

NOTES

Notes to Chapter 2

1 Costa & McCrae (1992a).
2 Tupes & Christal (1961); Goldberg (1990, 1993).
3 Hahn, Lee, & Ashton (1999).
4 Boies, Lee, Ashton, Pascal, & Nicol (2001). For a summary of the findings across these languages, see Ashton, Lee, Perugini, Szarota, de Vries, Di Blas, et al. (2004).
5 Ashton, Lee, & Goldberg (2004).
6 Lee & Ashton (2008).
7 See De Raad et al. (2010) for the argument that neither six nor five factors can be fully recovered across these languages; for responses see Ashton & Lee (2010), Ashton, Lee, & de Vries (2012), Saucier (2009).
8 The Emotionality factor of the HEXACO model is similar but not identical to the Big Five Neuroticism factor. We decided that Emotionality was a more accurate label, and it made for a very nice acronym. By the way, don't take the names of the factors too seriously. The names are convenient, but they oversimplify; you can understand the factors better by knowing the traits that belong to them.

Notes to Chapter 3

1 Because these strategies are personality dispositions rather than conscious choices, people aren't completely free to change their strategies according to the circumstances they face. Although people can try to adjust their behaviour according to the conditions they encounter, this may be very difficult (though not impossible) when the behaviour is inconsistent with their personality disposition.
2 High-O people tend to know more facts and words than low-O people. But this difference isn't because high-O people are any smarter in general than low-O people. On average, people low in

O are just as good as people high in O at solving difficult problems in logic or math. But because high-O people tend to read widely and enjoy learning new things, on average they learn more facts and words than low-O people do.

3 Some researchers have suggested that high O also carries the risk of developing certain very harmful mental illnesses, such as schizophrenia or other delusional disorders. However, the link between O and these disorders is very weak (Ashton & Lee, 2012) and probably contributes very little to the total cost of being high in O.

4 Aiello & Wheeler (1995).

5 These advantages of high C don't have anything to do with intelligence: high-C people aren't any smarter, on average, than low-C people. Now, smarter people—as identified by well-validated IQ tests—do achieve better grades and do perform better on the job, just as high-C people do. But because IQ and C are uncorrelated with each other, we can predict people's school and job performance much better by knowing their levels both of IQ *and* of C than by knowing either alone. The best performers are high in both C and IQ, and the worst are low in both; people who are high in C but low in IQ, or low in C but high in IQ, are in between.

6 Gailliot & Baumeister (2007).

7 Some researchers have suggested that because high-C individuals aren't impulsive, they lack spontaneity and are too slow in seizing good opportunities. But this suggestion confuses two quite different kinds of impulsivity. The inability to control one's impulses is associated with low C. But the readiness to seize opportunities is actually associated with *high* C (at least to a weak extent) and with high X (to a stronger extent); see Dickman (1990).

8 In case you were wondering, high-X and low-X individuals can be described pretty accurately by the common terms "extraverted" and "introverted."

9 This raises the interesting question of how it is that high-X people are viewed as more attractive. Perhaps physically attractive people

tend to develop higher levels of X as a result of the positive social attention they receive. Or perhaps high-X people are perceived as more attractive because of their vitality and sociability. Or maybe high-X people actually *behave* in ways that make them more attractive—even in their objective physical appearance—for example, by being more physically active or more interested in improving their appearance.

10 The costs and benefits of being high in X also depend on other people's levels of this dimension. If most people are low in X, then a high-X person may easily attract friends, allies, and mates. But if most people are high in X, then a high-X person will be only one of many potentially attractive social partners. In such a case, the benefits of high X may be too small to justify the energy costs and risks, and people low in X will have an advantage for survival and reproduction.

11 People sometimes express surprise that traits of honesty and humility go together in the same category. But lack of humility and lack of honesty are part of the same tendency to exploit other people: persons who have a strong sense of superiority and entitlement tend to feel justified in using deceit and manipulation to get what they want from others.

12 This is not to say that high-H people consciously think in terms of these consequences. A truly high-H person is governed by a sense of personal ethics that makes him or her behave *as if* any act of exploiting others would be punished—as it will be, by the person's own conscience—even when there is objectively no chance of being detected or of suffering retaliation.

13 For marital satisfaction, see Watson et al. (2004); for heart disease, see Chida & Steptoe (2009).

14 Cohen et al. (1996).

15 The costs and benefits of being high or low in A probably depend on the trait levels of other people. What matters here isn't so much the levels of A that other people have, but rather their levels of H.

When many people are low in H, then a low level of A can be better, because anger and resentment can help protect you from people who are inclined to exploit you. But when people are generally high in H, a high level of A can be better, because it's safe to err on the side of tolerance when you're dealing with people who are basically fair-minded. Likewise, the costs and benefits of high versus low H also depend on the levels of H that other people have. When almost no one else is low in H, a low-H person may exploit others rather successfully, but when many people are low in H, it may become much harder to do so.

16 See Silove, Marnane, Wagner, Manicavasagar, and Rees (2010) for links between adult separation anxiety disorder and personality traits related to Emotionality.

17 Ashton, Lee, Visser, & Pozzebon (2008).

18 Campbell (1999); Taylor et al. (2000).

19 Bouchard & Loehlin (2001); Loehlin (2005); Plomin & Caspi (1999); Riemann, Angleitner, & Strelau (1997); Riemann & Kandler (2010); Kandler, Riemann, Spinath, & Angleitner (2010). For a discussion of common misconceptions about heritability studies, see Visscher, Hill, and Wray (2008).

20 For some other psychological traits—such as intelligence, religious beliefs, and political attitudes—differences between households do contribute heavily to differences between people—but only until adolescence or early adulthood. Apparently, the household in which one is raised will have some influence on one's IQ and beliefs and attitudes, but that influence becomes quite weak after early adulthood (Plomin & Spinath, 2004). We explore this further in Chapter 7, in discussing political attitudes.

21 Harris (1995).

22 Sulloway (1995).

23 Jefferson, Herbst, & McCrae (1998); Loehlin (1997).

24 Roberts, Walton, & Viechtbauer (2006).

25 For those of you who like numbers, the estimated correlation across this 50-year span is about .60 to .80. Although this value is very high,

it also means that at least a few people undergo important changes in personality, relative to their age peers. For example, people who have experienced an episode of major depression—generally brought about by some crisis in their lives—tend to show larger shifts in levels of some personality traits, such as Extraversion or Emotionality. See Costa & McCrae (1992b).

Notes to Chapter 4

1 Ashton, Lee, Pozzebon, Visser, & Worth (2010). Note that many forms of risk taking are not status driven, but are motivated instead by the sensations of the experience itself—consider, for example, outdoor adventures such as mountain climbing or deep-sea diving. This kind of adventure seeking depends on several personality factors in combination—low E, high X, high O, and low C, with only a weak element of low H (see, for example, de Vries, de Vries, & Feij, 2009; Lee, Ogunfowora, & Ashton, 2005; Weller & Tikir, 2011).

2 Kruger & Nesse (2004); Kruger (2007); Daly & Wilson (2001); Wilson & Daly (1985); Frank & Cook (1995).

3 Lee, Ogunfowora, & Ashton (2005).

4 Bourdage, Lee, Ashton, & Perry (2007).

5 Schmitt & Buss (2000).

6 See Buss (1989) for sex differences in mate preferences.

7 Lee & Ashton (2012).

8 Rubenzer & Faschingbauer (2004).

9 This particular Five-Factor Model questionnaire (Costa & McCrae, 1992a) includes an Agreeableness scale that incorporates some aspects of HEXACO Agreeableness, Honesty-Humility, and Emotionality (see Ashton & Lee, 2005), and a Neuroticism scale that incorporates some aspects of HEXACO Emotionality and (low) Agreeableness. Other aspects of HEXACO Honesty-Humility and Emotionality are not so well accommodated by this questionnaire.

10 Johnson (1998).

11 Godbold (2010).

12 Marcus, Lee, & Ashton (2007).

13 See Williams, Paulhus, & Hare (2007).

14 De Vries, Lee, & Ashton (2008).

15 Gottfredson & Hirschi (1990).

16 Our colleague Bernd Marcus has discussed some key issues in measuring self-control, the central trait of the general theory of crime; Marcus (2004).

17 Ashton & Lee (2008).

18 Bourdage, Lee, Ashton, & Perry (2007).

19 Twigger (2010) found that problem gamblers tended to be low in H and C, and also low in E.

20 Blickle, Schlegel, Fassbender, & Klein (2006).

21 The most serious criminal offenders—serial killers, for example— will likely combine low H with low C as well as low E and low A. But according to forensic psychologists, a few serial killers are particularly orderly and disciplined. These so-called "macho man" serial killers (who may appear to function well within military or law enforcement settings) would seem to be extremely low in H and E and A, but rather high in C.

22 Haney, Banks, & Zimbardo (1973).

23 Zimbardo, Maslach & Haney (2000).

24 Carnahan & McFarland (2007).

25 Ashton & Lee (2008).

26 Ashton & Lee (2008); Lee et al. (2008).

27 See Alan Sokal and Jean Bricmont's (1998) *Intellectual Impostures* for a criticism of the pretentious but nonsensical writings of several postmodernists.

Notes to Chapter 5

1 Vazire, Naumann, Rentfrow, & Gosling (2008).

2 By the way, there's another objection to the use of self-reports to measure H, although we've never heard anyone mention it: you

could argue that humble people will never claim to be humble in self-report questionnaires, because their very humility will forbid them from doing so. But in fact, high-H people do reveal their humility, as for example when they state that they *don't* consider themselves to be any better or more deserving than others.

3 Noftle & Robins (2007); Anderson, John, Keltner, & Kring (2001).

4 Roberts, Kuncel, Shiner, Caspi, & Goldberg (2007).

5 See Funder, Kolar, & Blackman (1995); Costa & McCrae (1992a); Lee & Ashton (2006).

6 Paulhus, Bruce, & Trapnell (1995).

7 Borkenau & Liebler (1992).

8 However, there is one trait within the H factor that *doesn't* show particularly strong agreement between self-reports and observer reports, even when the observer is the spouse. Specifically, people's self-reports of sincerity or straightforwardness—of the tendency not to engage in subtle manipulation, such as flattery or false friendliness—are only modestly correlated with observer reports of these traits. Apparently, people who subtly manipulate others really are subtle about it, to the extent that even their spouses have only a roughly accurate sense of how much they do this.

9 Bolino & Turnley (1999).

Notes to Chapter 6

1 White (1980).

2 Lykken & Tellegen (1993); Watson et al. (2004).

3 It's interesting to speculate about the trait of intelligence in this context of selecting mates. Does it behave like physical attractiveness (the more, the better), or like religiosity (the more like me, the better)? Studies show that spouses tend to be similar in some but not all aspects of intelligence: they're usually similar in verbal ability (their vocabulary, general knowledge, etc.) but not necessarily in mathematical ability. But it isn't clear whether this similarity in verbal ability results from a competitive marketplace situation,

whereby people implicitly try to get someone as verbally smart as they possibly can, or simply from a preference for people similar to oneself. (Either way, it makes sense that spouses would be more similar in verbal ability than in mathematical ability: most couples spend a lot of time in conversation with each other, but only the nerdiest couples would spend any time doing math together.)

4 Feng & Baker (1994).

5 Actually, another way to examine similarity would be to compare Jack's observer report about Jill with Jill's observer report about Jack. This method generally gives results similar to those based on comparisons of self-reports.

6 Lee, Ashton, Pozzebon, Visser, Bourdage, & Ogunfowora (2009).

7 As noted earlier, our participant samples consisted mainly of friendship pairs, but there were also many romantic couples, including even a few married couples, as well as some sibling pairs and other pairs of relatives. But because most of our participant pairs consisted of two friends, we'll describe the results here in terms of friendship pairs. The results were generally about the same, by the way, for the romantic couples and for the pairs of relatives.

8 Schwartz (1992).

9 This importance of personal values also helps to explain why perceived similarity is stronger than actual similarity. For example, what matters when Jill forms or maintains a social relationship with Jack is not how similar to her Jack really is, but how similar Jill *thinks* Jack is.

10 Of course, this would depend on that person having a large enough circle of people to choose friends from—it might not work for people living in a small community where the choice of friends is limited.

Notes to Chapter 7

1 Note that this isn't the case for other matters of opinion or taste that lack any element of values. For example, "morning people" and "evening people" are unlikely to feel much discomfort about this

difference between them, nor are "dog people" and "cat people," or "tea people" and "coffee people," and so on.

2 Altemeyer (1981, 1996).

3 Pratto, Sidanius, Stallworth, & Malle (1994).

4 The terms "left-wing" and "right-wing" have a similar meaning across countries. However, the terms "liberal" and "conservative" differ in meaning between Europe and North America. Here we use the North American meanings, whereby "liberal" and "conservative" are more or less interchangeable with "left-wing" and "right-wing," respectively.

5 Federico, Hunt, & Ergun (2009).

6 Schlenker, Chambers, & Le (2012).

7 Duckitt, Wagner, du Plessis, & Birum (2002); McFarland (2005).

8 Altemeyer (2004, 2006).

9 Lee, Ashton, Ogunfowora, Bourdage, & Shin (2010).

10 Koenig et al. (2005); Eaves et al. (1997).

11 Pew Research Center for the People and the Press (2009).

12 Nakhaie & Brym (1999).

13 Data from Goldberg's Oregon sample.

14 See Nakhaie & Brym (1999).

15 Carney, Jost, Gosling, & Potter (2008).

16 http://www.cnn.com/ELECTION/2008/results/polls/#val=USP00p3

17 Lippa (2005).

18 Lewis & Seaman (2004).

19 Hodson, Hogg, & MacInnis (2009); Lee et al. (2010).

20 Son Hing, Bobocel, Zanna, & McBride (2007).

21 Duriez, Soenens, & Vansteenkiste (2008).

22 See McFarland, Ageyev, & Abalakina-Paap (1992) for a discussion of right-wing authoritarianism in the Soviet Union.

23 Chirumbolo & Leone (2010); Zettler & Hilbig (2010); Zettler, Hilbig, & Haubrich (2011).

24 Some studies indicate a role for the C factor in political party support: people higher in C are slightly more likely to favour right-wing political parties. Presumably, the policies typically espoused

by those parties—for example, favouring stricter law enforcement or economic self-reliance—have somewhat weaker appeal to low-C persons, who are more impulsive and less hard working.

Notes to Chapter 8

1 Here we'll treat as religions only those ethical or philosophical systems that are based on supernatural beliefs. Note, however, that for some people in modern societies, religion primarily represents a cultural or ethnic affiliation that is now largely independent of any supernatural beliefs—consider, for example, the many secular Jews who retain a strong sense of Jewish identity. Note also that some movements widely viewed as religions do not necessarily involve any supernatural elements. One example is Confucianism, which provides a way of life without prescribing any particular supernatural forces. However, even Confucianism is practised within the traditions of Chinese folk religion, which does include supernatural beliefs.

2 Lee, Ogunfowora, & Ashton (2005).

3 Saroglou (2010). Saroglou also found that religious people tended to be a bit higher in the C factor—to be more disciplined and organized. This suggests that religions tend to attract and retain high-C people—who presumably are better able to follow the ordered lifestyle that is prescribed by religious teachings—or to promote high-C tendencies in their followers.

4 Wink, Ciciolla, Dillon, & Tracy (2007).

5 The tendency for soft-hearted people to be a bit more religious is true even if we consider either sex alone: soft-hearted men are slightly more likely to be religious than are hard-hearted men, and the same is true among women.

6 Brooks (2006).

7 The link between religiosity and the H factor in particular shows up in an interesting way in unpublished data from Goldberg's sample of Oregon residents. One of the surveys administered to that sample asked about the respondents' possessions. Among the findings of

that survey was that high-H people tended to own more religious books—such as the Bible—than did low-H people. In contrast, low-H people owned more cellphones, credit cards, and bottles of liquor than did high-H people. The correlations were not very strong, however: many high-H people do own cellphones and credit cards and bottles of liquor and don't own a Bible.

8 http://people-press.org/report/?pageid=1549

9 Larson & Witham (1997, 1998).

10 See Nyborg (2009). Nyborg confined the analyses to teenagers who were White and non-Hispanic, so that any racial or ethnic differences would not influence the results.

11 Saucier & Skrzypińska (2006).

12 Note that traditional religious beliefs and mystical spiritual beliefs are unrelated to each other—they're not opposite to each other. Some people are both traditionally religious and mystically spiritual and hence accept both kinds of supernatural beliefs described above. And some people are neither traditionally religious nor mystically spiritual, rejecting all supernatural beliefs.

13 Data from Goldberg's sample of Oregon residents.

14 For a detailed discussion, see Wilson (2002, pp. 134–135).

Notes to Chapter 9

1 The link between H and theft is found across different countries: in a study with our colleague Reinout de Vries, we found similar results for college students in Canada, Australia, and the Netherlands (Lee, Ashton, & de Vries, 2005).

2 Hershfield, Cohen, & Thompson (2012).

3 Ashton & Lee (2008); Lee, Ashton, Morrison, Cordery, & Dunlop (2008).

4 Smith (1776).

5 Hilbig, Zettler, & Heydasch (2012).

6 Frank (1999).

7 Book, Volk, & Hosker (2012).

8 Bourdage, Lee, Ashton, & Perry (2007).
9 Ashton & Lee (2008); see also Lee, Gizzarone, & Ashton (2003).
10 See Frank (1999) for a progressive consumption tax.

Notes to Chapter 10

1   Twigger (2010).

REFERENCES

Aiello, L.C., & Wheeler, P. (1995). The expensive-tissue hypothesis: The brain and the digestive system in human and primate evolution. *Current Anthropology, 36*, 199–221.

Altemeyer, B. (1981). *Right-wing authoritarianism*. Winnipeg: University of Manitoba Press.

Altemeyer, B. (1996). *The authoritarian specter*. Cambridge, MA: Harvard University Press.

Altemeyer, B. (2004). Highly dominating, highly authoritarian personalities. *Journal of Social Psychology, 144*, 421–447.

Altemeyer, B. (2006). *The Authoritarians*. Winnipeg: Author.

Anderson, C., John, O.P., Keltner, D., & Kring, A.M. (2001). Who attains social status? Effects of personality and physical attractiveness in social groups. *Journal of Personality and Social Psychology, 81*, 116–132.

Ashton, M.C., & Lee, K. (2005). Honesty-Humility, the Big Five, and the Five-Factor Model. *Journal of Personality, 73*, 1321–1353.

Ashton, M.C., & Lee, K. (2008). The prediction of honesty-humility-related criteria by the HEXACO and Five-Factor models of personality. *Journal of Research in Personality, 42,* 1216–1228.

Ashton, M.C., & Lee, K. (2010). On the cross-language replicability of personality factors. *Journal of Research in Personality, 44*, 436–441.

Ashton, M.C., & Lee, K. (2012). Oddity, schizotypy/dissociation, and personality. *Journal of Personality, 80*, 113–134.

Ashton, M.C., Lee,K., & de Vries, R.E. (2012). *A consideration of two objections to the HEXACO model of personality structure*. Unpublished manuscript.

Ashton, M.C., Lee, K., & Goldberg, L.R. (2004). A hierarchical analysis of 1,710 English personality-descriptive adjectives. *Journal of Personality and Social Psychology, 87*, 707–721.

Ashton, M.C., Lee, K., Perugini, M., Szarota, P., de Vries, R. E., Di Blas, L., Boies, K., & De Raad, B. (2004). A six-factor structure of personality-descriptive adjectives: Solutions from psycholexical studies in seven languages. *Journal of Personality and Social Psychology, 86*, 356–366.

Ashton, M.C., Lee, K., Pozzebon, J.A., Visser, B.A., & Worth, N.C. (2010). Status-driven risk taking and the major dimensions of personality. *Journal of Research in Personality, 44*, 734–737.

Ashton, M.C., Lee, K., Visser, B.A., & Pozzebon, J.A. (2008). Phobic tendency within the HEXACO and Five-Factor Models of personality structure. *Journal of Research in Personality, 42*, 734–746.

Blickle, G., Schlegel, A., Fassbender, P., & Klein, U. (2006). Some personality correlates of white collar crime. *Applied Psychology: An International Review, 55*, 220–233.

Boies, K., Lee K., Ashton, M.C., Pascal, S., & Nicol, A.A.M. (2001). The structure of the French personality lexicon. *European Journal of Personality, 15*, 277–295.

Bolino, M.C., & Turnley, W.H. (1999). Measuring impression management in organizations: A scale development based on the Jones and Pittman taxonomy. *Organizational Research Methods, 2,* 187–206.

Book, A.S., Volk, A.A., & Hosker, A. (2012). Adolescent bullying and personality: An adaptive approach. *Personality and Individual Differences, 52*, 218–223.

Borkenau, P., & Liebler, A. (1992). Trait inferences: Sources of validity at zero-acquaintance. *Journal of Personality and Social Psychology, 62*, 645–657.

Bouchard, T. J., & Loehlin, J. C. (2001). Genes, evolution, and personality. *Behavior Genetics, 31,* 243-273.

Bourdage, J.S., Lee, K., Ashton, M.C., & Perry, A. (2007). Big Five and HEXACO model of personality correlates of sexuality. *Personality and Individual Differences, 43,* 1506–1516.

Brooks, A.C. (2006). *Who really cares: The surprising truth about compassionate conservatism.* New York: Basic Books.

Buss, D.M. (1989). Sex differences in human mate preferences: Evolutionary hypotheses tested in 37 cultures. *Behavioral and Brain Sciences, 12*, 1–49.

Campbell, A. (1999). Staying alive: Evolution, culture, and women's intrasexual aggression. *Behavioral and Brain Sciences, 22*, 223–252.

Carnahan, T., & McFarland, S. (2007). Revisiting the Stanford prison experiment: Could participant self-selection have led to the cruelty? *Personality and Social Psychology Bulletin, 55*, 603–614.

Carney, D.R., Jost, J.T., Gosling, S.D., & Potter, J. (2008). The secret lives of liberals and conservatives: Personality profiles, interaction styles, and the things they leave behind. *Political Psychology, 29*, 807–840.

Chida, Y., & Steptoe, A. (2009). The association of anger and hostility with future coronary heart disease: A meta-analytic review of prospective evidence. *Journal of the American College of Cardiology, 53*, 936–946.

Chirumbolo, A., & Leone, L. (2010). Personality and politics: The role of the HEXACO model in predicting personality and voting. *Personality and Individual Differences, 49*, 43–48.

Cohen, D., Nisbett, R.E., Bowdle, R.F., & Schwarz, N. (1996). Insult, aggression, and the "Southern culture of honor": An experimental ethnography. *Journal of Personality and Social Psychology, 70*, 945–960.

Costa, P.T., Jr., & McCrae, R.R. (1992a). *NEO Personality Inventory–Revised (NEO-PI-R) and NEO Five-Factor Inventory (NEO-FFI) Professional Manual*. Odessa, FL: Psychological Assessment Resources.

Costa, P.T., Jr., & McCrae, R.R. (1992b). Trait psychology comes of age. In T.B. Sonderegger (Ed.), *Nebraska Symposium on Motivation 1991: Psychology and Aging. Current Theory and Research in Motivation* (Vol. 39) (pp. 169–204). Lincoln, NE: University of Nebraska Press.

Daly, M., & Wilson, M. (2001). Risk-taking, intrasexual competition, and homicide. *Nebraska Symposium on Motivation, 47*, 1–36.

De Raad, B., Barelds, D.P.H., Levert, E., Ostendorf, F., Mlacic, B., Di Blas, L., et al. (2010). Only three factors of personality description are fully replicable across languages: A comparison of fourteen trait taxonomies. *Journal of Personality and Social Psychology, 98*, 160–173.

De Vries, R.E., De Vries, A., & Feij, J.A. (2009). Sensation seeking, risk taking, and the HEXACO model of personality. *Personality and Individual Differences, 47*, 536–540.

De Vries, R.E., Lee, K., & Ashton, M.C. (2008). The Dutch HEXACO Personality Inventory: Psychometric properties, self–other agreement and relations with psychopathy among low and high acquaintanceship dyads. *Journal of Personality Assessment, 90*, 142–151.

Dickman, S.J. (1990). Functional and dysfunctional impulsivity: Personality and cognitive correlates. *Journal of Personality and Social Psychology, 58*, 95–102.

Duckitt, J., Wagner, C., du Plessis, I., & Birum, I. (2002). The psychological bases of ideology and prejudice: Testing a dual process model. *Journal of Personality and Social Psychology, 83*, 75–93.

Duriez, B., Soenens, B., & Vansteenkiste, M. (2008). The intergenerational transmission of authoritarianism: The mediating role of parental goal promotion. *Journal of Research in Personality, 42*, 622–642.

Eaves, L., Martin, N., Heath, A., Schieken, R., Meyer, J., Silberg, J., Neale, M., & Corey, L. (1997). Age changes in the causes of individual differences in conservatism. *Behavioral Genetics, 27*, 121–124.

Federico, C.M., Hunt, C.V., & Ergun, D. (2009). Political expertise, social worldviews, and ideology: Translating "competitive jungles" and "dangerous worlds" into ideological reality. *Social Justice Research, 22*, 259–279.

Feng, D., & Baker, L.A. (1994). Spouse similarity in attitudes, personalities, and psychological well-being of American couples. *Behavior Genetics, 24*, 357–364.

Frank, R.H. (1999). *Luxury fever: Why money fails to satisfy in an era of excess*. New York: Free Press.

Frank, R.H., & Cook, P.J. (1995). *The winner-take-all society*. New York: Free Press.

Funder, D.C., Kolar, D.W., & Blackman, M.C. (1995). Agreement among judges of personality: Interpersonal relations, similarity, and acquaintanceship. *Journal of Personality and Social Psychology, 69*, 656–672.

Gailliot, M.T., & Baumeister, R.F. (2007). The physiology of willpower: Linking blood glucose to self-control. *Personality and Social Psychology Review, 11,* 303–327.

Godbold, E.S. (2010). *Jimmy and Rosalynn Carter: The Georgia Years 1924–1974*. New York: Oxford University Press.

Goldberg, L. R. (1990). An alternative "description of personality": The Big-Five factor structure. *Journal of Personality and Social Psychology, 59*, 1216–1229.

Goldberg, L. R. (1993). The structure of phenotypic personality traits. *American Psychologist, 48*, 26–34.

Gottfredson, M.R., & Hirschi, T. (1990). *A general theory of crime*. Stanford, CA: Stanford University Press.

Hahn, D.-W., Lee, K., & Ashton, M.C. (1999). A factor analysis of the most frequently used Korean personality trait adjectives. *European Journal of Personality, 13*, 261–282.

Haney, C., Banks, C., & Zimbardo, P. (1973). Interpersonal dynamics in a simulated prison. *International Journal of Criminology and Penology, 1*, 69–97.

Harris, J.R. (1995). *The nurture assumption: Why children turn out the way they do*. New York: Free Press.

Hershfield, H.E., Cohen, T.R., & Thompson, L. (2012). Short horizon and tempting situations: Lack of continuity to our future selves leads to unethical decision making and behaviour. *Organizational Behavior and Human Decision Processes, 117*, 298–310.

Hilbig, B.E., Zettler, I., & Heydasch, T. (2012). Personality, punishment, and public goods: Strategic shifts toward cooperation as a matter of dispositional Honesty-Humility. *European Journal of Personality, 26*, 245–254.

Hodson, G., Hogg, S.M., & MacInnis, C.C. (2009). The role of "dark personalities" (narcissism, Machiavellianism, psychopathy), Big Five personality factors, and ideology in explaining prejudice. *Journal of Research in Personality, 43,* 686–690.

Jefferson, T., Jr., Herbst, J.H., & McCrae, R.R. (1998). Associations between birth order and personality traits: Evidence from self-reports and observer ratings. *Journal of Research in Personality, 32,* 498–509.

Johnson, P. (1998). *A history of the American people.* New York: HarperCollins.

Kandler, C., Riemann, R., Spinath, F.M., & Angleitner, A. (2010). Sources of variance in personality facets: A multiple-rater twin study of self-peer, peer-peer, and self-self (dis)agreement. *Journal of Personality, 78,* 1565-1594.

Koenig, L.B., McGue, M., Krueger, R.F., & Bouchard, T.J., Jr. (2005). Genetic and environmental influences on religiousness: Findings for retrospective and current religiousness ratings. *Journal of Personality, 73,* 471–488.

Kruger, D.J. (2007). Economic transition, male competition, and sex differences in mortality rates. *Evolutionary Psychology, 5,* 411–427.

Kruger, D.J., & Nesse, R.M. (2004). Sexual selection and the male:female mortality ratio. *Evolutionary Psychology, 2,* 66–85.

Larson, J., & Witham, L. (1997). Scientists are still keeping the faith. *Nature, 386,* 435–436.

Larson, J., & Witham, L. (1998). Leading scientists still reject god. *Nature,* 394, 313.

Lee, K., & Ashton, M.C. (2006). Further assessment of the HEXACO Personality Inventory: Two new facet scales and an observer report form. *Psychological Assessment 18,* 182–191.

Lee, K., & Ashton, M.C. (2008). The HEXACO personality factors in the indigenous personality lexicons of English and 11 other languages. *Journal of Personality, 76,* 1001–1053.

Lee, K., & Ashton, M.C. (2012). Getting mad and getting even: Agreeableness and Honesty-Humility as predictors of revenge intentions. *Personality and Individual Differences, 52,* 596–600.

Lee, K., Ashton, M.C., & de Vries, R.E. (2005). Predicting workplace delinquency and integrity with the HEXACO and Five-Factor Models of personality structure. *Human Performance, 18,* 179–197.

Lee, K., Ashton, M.C., Morrison, D.L., Cordery, J., & Dunlop, P. (2008). Predicting integrity with the HEXACO personality model: Use of self- and observer reports. *Journal of Occupational and Organizational Psychology, 81,* 147–167.

Lee, K., Ashton, M.C., Ogunfowora, B., Bourdage, J., & Shin, K.-H. (2010). The personality bases of socio-political attitudes: The role of honesty-humility and openness to experience. *Journal of Research in Personality, 44*, 115–119.

Lee, K., Ashton, M.C., Pozzebon, J.A., Visser, B.A., Bourdage, J.S., & Ogunfowora, B. (2009). Similarity and assumed similarity of personality reports of well-acquainted persons. *Journal of Personality and Social Psychology, 96,* 460–472.

Lee, K., Gizzarone, M., & Ashton, M.C. (2003). Personality and the likelihood to sexually harass. *Sex Roles, 49,* 59–69.

Lee, K., Ogunfowora, B., & Ashton, M.C. (2005). Personality traits beyond the Big Five: Are they within the HEXACO space? *Journal of Personality, 73*, 1437–1463.

Lewis, G.B., & Seaman, B.A. (2004). Sexual orientation and demand for the arts. *Social Science Quarterly, 85*, 523–538.

Lippa, R. (2005). Sexual orientation and personality. *Annual Review of Sex Research, 16*, 119–153.

Loehlin, J.C. (1997). A test of J.R. Harris's theory of peer influences in personality. *Journal of Personality and Social Psychology, 72*, 1197–1201.

Loehlin, J.C. (2005). Resemblance in personality and attitudes between parents and their children: Genetic and environmental contributions. In S. Bowles, H. Gintis, & M. Osborne Groves (Eds.), *Unequal chances: Family background and economic success* (pp. 192–207). Princeton, NJ: Princeton University Press.

Lykken, D.T., & Tellegen, A. (1993). Is human mating adventitious or the result of lawful choice? A twin study of mate selection. *Journal of Personality and Social Psychology, 65*, 56–68.

Marcus, B. (2004). Self-control in the general theory of crime: Theoretical implications of a measurement problem. *Theoretical Criminology, 8*, 33–55.

Marcus, B., Lee, K., & Ashton, M.C. (2007). Personality dimensions explaining relationships between integrity tests and counterproductive behavior: Big Five, or one in addition? *Personnel Psychology, 60*, 1–34.

McFarland, S.G. (2005). On the eve of war: Authoritarianism, social dominance, and American students' attitudes toward attacking Iraq. *Personality and Social Psychology Bulletin, 31*, 360–367.

McFarland, S.G., Ageyev, V.S., & Abalakina-Paap, M. (1992). Authoritarianism in the former Soviet Union. *Journal of Personality and Social Psychology, 63,* 1004–1010.

Nakhaie, M.R., & Brym, R.J. (1999). The political attitudes of Canadian professors. *Canadian Journal of Sociology, 24*, 329–353.

Noftle, E.E., Robins, R.W. (2007). Personality predictors of academic outcomes: Big Five correlates of GPA and SAT scores. *Journal of Personality and Social Psychology, 93*, 116–130.

Nyborg, H. (2009). The intelligence–religiosity nexus: A representative study of white adolescent Americans. *Intelligence, 37*, 81–93.

Paulhus, D.L., Bruce, M.N., & Trapnell, P.D. (1995). Effects of self-presentation strategies on personality profiles and their structure. *Personality and Social Psychology Bulletin, 21*, 100–108.

Pew Research Center for the People and the Press (2009). *Public praises science: Scientists fault public, media.* Retrieved online from http://people-press.org/reports/pdf/528.pdf

Plomin, R., & Caspi, A. (1999). Behavioral genetics and personality. In L.A. Pervin & O.P. John (Eds.), *Handbook of Personality: Theory and research* (2nd ed.) (pp. 251–276). New York: Guilford Press.

Plomin, R., & Spinath, F.M. (2004). Intelligence: Genetics, genes, and genomics. *Journal of Personality and Social Psychology, 86*, 112–129.

Pratto, F., Sidanius, J., Stallworth, L.M., & Malle, B.F. (1994). Social dominance orientation: A personality variable predicting social and political attitudes. *Journal of Personality and Social Psychology, 67*, 741–763.

Riemann, R., Angleitner, A., & Strelau, J. (1997). Genetic and environmental influences on personality: A study of twins reared together using the self- and peer-report NEO-FFI scales. *Journal of Personality, 65*, 449–475.

Riemann, R., & Kandler, C. (2010). Construct validation using multitrait-multimethod twin data: The case of a general factor of personality. *European Journal of Personality, 78*, 1565–1594.

Roberts, B.W., Kuncel, N.R., Shiner, R., Caspi, A., & Goldberg, L.R. (2007). The power of personality: The comparative validity of personality traits, socioeconomic status, and cognitive ability for predicting important life outcomes. *Perspective on Psychological Science, 2*, 313–345.

Roberts, B.W., Walton, K.E., & Viechtbauer, W. (2006). Patterns of mean-level change in personality traits across the life course: A meta-analysis of longitudinal studies. *Psychological Bulletin, 132*, 1–25.

Rubenzer, S.J., & Faschingbauer, T.R. (2004). *Personality, character, and leadership in the White House: Psychologists assess the presidents.* Washington, DC: Brassey's.

Saucier, G. (2009). Recurrent personality dimensions in inclusive lexical studies: Indications for a Big Six structure. *Journal of Personality, 77*, 1577–1614.

Saucier, G., & Skrzypińska, K. (2006). Spiritual but not religious? Evidence for two independent dimensions. *Journal of Personality, 74*, 1257–1292.

Saroglou, V. (2010). Religiousness as a cultural adaptation of basic traits: A five-factor model perspective. *Personality and Social Psychology Review, 14*, 108–125.

Schlenker, B.R., Chambers, J.R., & Le, B.M. (2012). Conservatives are happier than liberals, but why? Political ideology, personality, and life satisfaction. *Journal of Research in Personality, 46*, 127–146.

Schmitt, D.P., & Buss, D.M. (2000). Sexual dimensions of person description: Beyond or subsumed by the Big Five? *Journal of Research in Personality, 34*, 141–177.

Schwartz, S. H. (1992). Universals in the content and structure of values: Theoretical advances and empirical tests in 20 countries. *Advances in Experimental Social Psychology, 25*, 1–65.

Silove, D.M., Marnane, C.L., Wagner, R., Manicavasagar, V.L., & Rees, S. (2010). The prevalence and correlates of adult separation anxiety disorder in an anxiety clinic. *BMC Psychiatry, 10*, 21.

Smith, A. (1776). *An inquiry into the nature and causes of the wealth of nations*. London: Strahan & Cadell.

Sokal, A., & Bricmont, J. (1998). *Intellectual impostures*. London: Profile Books.

Son Hing, L.S., Bobocel, D.R., Zanna, M.P., & McBride, M.V. (2007). Authoritarian dynamics and unethical decision making: High social dominance orientation leaders and high right-wing authoritarianism followers. *Journal of Personality and Social Psychology, 92*, 67–81.

Sulloway, F.J. (1996). *Born to rebel: Birth order, family dynamics, and creative lives*. New York: Pantheon.

Taylor, S.E., Klein, L.C., Lewis, B.P., Gruenewald, T.L., Gurung, R.A.R., & Updegraff, J.A. (2000). Biobehavioral responses to stress in females: Tend-and-befriend, not fight-or-flight. *Psychological Review, 107*, 411–429.

Tupes, E.C., & Christal, R.E. (1961). *Recurrent personality factors based on trait ratings* (USAF Tech. Rep. No. 61-97). US Air Force: Lackland Air Force Base, TX.

Twigger, K. (2010). *An examination of the role of personality and self-regulation in the gambling behaviours of late adolescents and emerging adults*. Unpublished master's thesis, Brock University, St. Catharines, ON.

Vazire, S., Naumann, L.P., Rentfrow, P.J., & Gosling S.D. (2008). Portrait of a narcissist: Manifestations of narcissism in physical appearance. *Journal of Research in Personality, 42*, 1439–1447.

Visscher, P.M., Hill, W.G., & Wray, N.R. (2008). Heritability in the genomics era—concepts and misconceptions. *Nature Reviews Genetics, 9*, 255–266.

Watson, D., Klohnen, E.C., Casillas, A., Simms, E., Haig, J., & Berry, D.S. (2004). Match makers and deal breakers: Analyses of assortative mating in newlywed couples. *Journal of Personality, 72*, 1029–1068.

Weller, J.A., & Tikir, A. (2011). Predicting domain-specific risk taking with the HEXACO personality structure. *Journal of Behavioral Decision Making, 24*, 180–201.

White, G.L. (1980). Physical attractiveness and courtship progress. *Journal of Persoanlity and Social Psychology, 39*, 660–668.

Williams, K.M., Paulhus, D.L., & Hare, R.D. (2007). Capturing the four-facet structure of psychopathy in college students via self-report. *Journal of Personality Assessment, 88*, 205–219.

Wilson, D.S. (2002). *Darwin's Cathedral: Evolution, religion, and the nature of society*. Chicago: University of Chicago Press.

Wilson, M., & Daly, M. (1985). Competitiveness, risk taking, and violence: The young male syndrome. *Ethology and Sociobiology, 6*, 59–73.

Wink, P., Ciciolla, L., Dillon, M., & Tracy, A. (2007). Religiousness, spiritual seeking, and personality: Findings from a longitudinal study. *Journal of Personality, 75*, 1051–1070.

Zettler, I., & Hilbig, B.E. (2010). Attitudes of the selfless: Explaining political orientation with altruism. *Personality and Individual Differences, 48*, 338–342.

Zettler, I., Hilbig, B.E., & Haubrich, J. (2011). Altruism at the ballots: Predicting political attitudes and behavior. *Journal of Research in Personality, 45*, 130–133.

Zimbardo, P.G., Maslach, C., & Haney, C. (2000). Reflections on the Stanford prison experiment: Genesis, transformations, consequences. In T. Blass (Ed.), *Obedience to authority: Current perspectives on the Milgram paradigm* (pp. 193–237). Mahwah, NJ: Lawrence Erlbaum.